Data Analytics for Starters: World's Most Prospective Skill Simplified

Data Analytics for Starters: World's Most Prospective Skill Simplified

Copyright 2023, Micheal Lee

Contents

Introduction

Would you like to learn how to use data analytics to expand your company, streamline your operations, and improve your decision-making? If so, you should read this ebook!

You can learn the fundamentals of data analytics from data collection and cleaning to data visualization and modeling by reading Data Analytics for Starters, a thorough manual. To solve real-world issues and situations, you will learn how to apply data analytics techniques, including customer segmentation, product recommendation, sentiment analysis, and more. You can learn the concepts and skills in this ebook's clear, concise, and engaging writing style, which includes many examples and exercises. A companion website with code snippets, datasets, and additional resources will also be made available to you.

Data Analytics for Starters will make you a confident and skilled data analyst quickly, whether you are a beginner or an intermediate learner. Don't pass up this chance to harness the power of data analytics for your success in both your personal and professional life!

Chapter One: Why Is Data Analytics Important

Welcome to the world of data.

Businesses and organizations are producing enormous amounts of data at an unprecedented rate in the modern digital age. This data, which ranges from consumer transactions and website interactions to social media posts and sensor data, contains insightful information that can 8help decision-makers make well-informed choices and open up new possibilities. You would agree with me that companies of the world are now diving into data resources and looking the best way to manage the long ignored potentials of these awesome materials. In order to find significant patterns, trends, and insights data can be utilized to inform strategic decisions and enhance business outcomes. To do this, data must be examined, transformed, and modeled. This process is known as data analytics.

The Importance of Data Analytics

For a number of reasons, data analytics is becoming more and more crucial in today's workplaces and businesses. Let's examine some of the main causes for the rise in popularity of data analytics:

Data-Driven Decision Making

In the past, making decisions was largely based on experience and intuition. The availability of big and varied datasets has, however, allowed firms to make better informed choices based on data-driven facts and insights. Businesses may reduce uncertainty, spot trends, and make empirically supported strategic decisions by utilizing data.

Increased Effectiveness and Efficiency

Data analytics helps businesses streamline their procedures. Businesses can spot bottlenecks, inefficiencies, and places for improvement by evaluating data. This may result in improved production, decreased expenses, and simplified operations. For instance, a store can utilize data analytics to improve stock management and waste reduction by optimizing inventory levels and supply chain processes.

Enhanced Customer Understanding

The foundation of every organization is its customers. Utilizing data analytics, businesses can examine the preferences, activities, and demands of their customers to better understand them. Businesses can customize their offers, enhance consumer experiences, and more effectively target their marketing efforts with the help of this information. For instance, an online retailer can use client browsing and purchasing patterns to tailor product recommendations, increasing consumer satisfaction and loyalty.

Competitive Advantage

Data analytics can offer a sizable competitive edge in today's fiercely competitive environment. Effective data analysis enables businesses to recognize industry trends, find new opportunities, and move more quickly than rivals toward data-driven strategic decisions. They can take advantage of new trends, stay ahead of the curve, and react to shifting market conditions thanks to this. Companies like Netflix and Amazon have used data analytics to acquire a competitive edge and disrupt their respective sectors.

Predictive Risk Management

Data analytics is essential for identifying and reducing risks in a variety of businesses. Organizations can detect possible hazards and take proactive steps to prevent or minimize them by studying historical data and using predictive analytics approaches. Financial institutions, for instance, can utilize data analytics to identify trends and abnormalities in transaction data to identify fraudulent activity, hence reducing losses.

Improved Business Prospects

Data analytics can open up new perspectives and business prospects, which can lead to innovation. Organizations can find market opportunities, spot new trends, and create cutting-edge goods and services to satisfy shifting consumer expectations by analyzing data. Businesses can experiment and test new ideas with data analytics, which results in better goods, services, and business models.

Evaluation and Measurement of Performance

Data analytics enables firms to evaluate and quantify their performance in an unbiased manner. Businesses may track their progress, pinpoint areas for development, and adjust their strategy as necessary by defining pertinent metrics and evaluating data. This aids in evaluating the performance of efforts, establishing realistic targets, and efficiently allocating resources.

Summarily, the use of data analytics is very essential in today's workplaces and businesses. It enables data-driven decision-making, increases efficiency, helps businesses better understand their customers, gives them a competitive edge, reduces risks, encourages innovation, and measures success for companies. Organizations that leverage the potential of data analytics will be better able to manage the complexity of the business landscape, make educated decisions, and achieve sustainable growth as data continues to rise exponentially. As data continues to grow exponentially, organizations that harness the power of data analytics will be better equipped to navigate the complexities of the business landscape, make informed decisions, and achieve sustainable growth in the digital era.

For better understanding of the later discourse of this book we would look at key concepts and terminology in data analytics.

Data: Data refers to the raw, unprocessed facts and figures collected from various sources. It can be in the form of numbers, text, images, audio, or video.

Data Analytics: Data analytics involves the process of examining and interpreting data to extract meaningful insights, patterns, and trends. It encompasses various techniques, methodologies, and tools used to analyze data for decision-making purposes.

Descriptive Analytics: Descriptive analytics focuses on summarizing and describing historical data to understand what happened in the past. It includes techniques such as data aggregation, data visualization, and statistical analysis.

Predictive Analytics: Predictive analytics involves using historical data and statistical models to make predictions or forecasts about future events or outcomes. It utilizes techniques like regression analysis, time series analysis, and machine learning algorithms.

Prescriptive Analytics: Prescriptive analytics goes beyond predicting future outcomes and suggests the best course of action to achieve desired outcomes. It combines historical data, predictive models, and optimization techniques to provide recommendations for decision-making.

Exploratory Data Analysis (EDA): EDA is an approach to analyzing data that focuses on discovering patterns, relationships, and anomalies. It involves techniques such as data visualization, summary statistics, and data mining to gain initial insights into the data.

Data Mining: Data mining is the process of extracting valuable and actionable information from large datasets. It involves discovering hidden patterns, relationships, and trends in the data using techniques such as clustering, classification, and association rules.

Machine Learning: Machine learning is a branch of artificial intelligence that focuses on enabling computer systems to learn from data and improve performance without being explicitly programmed. It involves algorithms that automatically learn patterns and make predictions or decisions based on training data.

Regression Analysis: Regression analysis is a statistical technique used to model the relationship between a dependent variable and one or more independent variables. It helps in understanding how changes in independent variables impact the dependent variable.

Data Visualization: Data visualization is the graphical representation of data to visually communicate insights and patterns. It includes charts, graphs, maps, and other visual elements that make complex data more understandable and accessible.

Big Data: Big data refers to extremely large and complex datasets that are difficult to manage and process using traditional data processing methods. It typically involves high-volume, high-velocity, and high-variety data, often requiring specialized tools and technologies for analysis.

Data Cleaning: Data cleaning, also known as data cleansing or data scrubbing, involves the process of identifying and correcting errors, inconsistencies, and inaccuracies in the dataset. It ensures that the data used for analysis is reliable and accurate.

Data Transformation: Data transformation involves converting data from one format or structure to another to make it suitable for analysis. It includes tasks such as data normalization, aggregation, filtering, and feature engineering.

Data Warehouse: A data warehouse is a central repository that stores and integrates data from various sources within an organization. It provides a unified view of the data and supports efficient data analysis and reporting.

Data Governance: Data governance refers to the set of processes, policies, and controls that ensure the availability, integrity, and security of data within an organization. It establishes guidelines for data management, data quality, and data privacy.

Data Privacy: Data privacy concerns the protection of personal or sensitive information collected and stored by organizations. It involves implementing measures to safeguard data from unauthorized access, use, or disclosure.

Data Security: Data security focuses on protecting data from unauthorized access, alteration, or destruction. It involves implementing security measures such as encryption, access controls, and intrusion detection systems.

Becoming a Data Analyst

You will need a mix of abilities, education, and work experience to become a data analyst. The majority of data analysts has a bachelor's degree or higher in a subject that is connected to data analysis, such as math, statistics, computer science, economics, or engineering. For some jobs, especially those that are more advanced or specialized, a master's degree or higher may be necessary.

Skills in statistics and data analysis: It's essential to have a solid foundation in these fields. The principles of statistics, probability theory, hypothesis testing, regression analysis, and other analytical methods should be familiar to you. Understanding software for data manipulation and analysis, such as R or Python, is also crucial. Data retrieval, manipulation, and querying from databases all require a solid understanding of SQL (Structured Query Language). Data cleaning and transformation skills are also essential for data analysis activities.

The ability to visually exhibit data is crucial for sharing insights with key stakeholders. It is good to be familiar with Python libraries like Matplotlib or Seaborn as well as data visualization systems like Tableau, Power BI, or both.

Understanding several programming languages is helpful when analyzing data. Languages like Python and R are frequently utilized in the industry. You can automate monotonous operations, handle data, and create analytical models by being proficient in programming.

Understanding the field or industry in which you'll be working is advantageous. It aids in data interpretation and analysis within the confines of your specialized expertise. For instance, diverse domain expertise may be needed in the fields of healthcare, finance, marketing, or e-commerce.

Data analysts frequently deal with difficult challenges that need for analytical thinking and problem-solving skills. Finding solutions requires the ability to analyze issues, create hypotheses, and apply analytical methods. Data analysts must be able to successfully communicate their findings and insights to both technical and non-technical stakeholders. To convey material in an intelligible and straightforward way, one needs strong written and verbal communication abilities.

New tools, techniques, and technologies are continuously developed in the field of data analysis, which is a topic that is continually growing. For professional development, it's critical to be open to lifelong learning and to keep up with the newest developments. It will also be helpful to have knowledge with data analysis software and tools, such as Excel, SQL, Python, R, and statistical applications like SPSS or SAS. Your abilities can be improved by gaining practical experience using real-world data sets through internships, side projects, or freelance employment.

Keep in mind that the particular qualifications may change depending on the company, sector, or job position you're applying for. Your career as a data analyst will take off if you lay a solid foundation in these areas.

Chapter Two: Getting Started

Setting up Your Data Analytics Environment: Unleash the Power of Insights

In the ever-evolving world of data analytics, setting up a robust and efficient environment is essential to uncovering valuable insights that drive informed decision-making. By establishing the right tools, infrastructure, and processes, you can unleash the power of data and transform it into a strategic asset. Let's embark on a journey to create an exceptional data analytics environment that is detailed, enthusiastic, informative, and interesting.

Define Your Objectives:

To begin, clearly define your data analytics objectives. Understand the specific business problems you aim to solve and the insights you seek. Whether it's optimizing marketing campaigns, improving operational efficiency, or enhancing customer experience, having a well-defined purpose will shape your entire environment.

Assemble Your Data:

Data is the lifeblood of analytics, and ensuring its quality and accessibility is paramount. Gather relevant data from various sources, including databases, spreadsheets,

APIs, and third-party vendors. Consider the volume, velocity, and variety of data to determine the storage and processing requirements.

Choose the Right Platform:

Selecting the appropriate platform to aid your data analytics environment is crucial. Cloud-based solutions like Amazon Web Services (AWS), Microsoft Azure, or Google Cloud Platform offer scalability, flexibility, and cost-efficiency. Alternatively, on-premises solutions can provide greater control and security, depending on your organization's needs.

Data Integration and ETL Processes:

Efficiently integrating and transforming data is a fundamental step in data analytics. Implement Extract, Transform, Load (ETL) processes to clean, normalize, and combine disparate data sources. Leverage tools like Apache Spark, Informatica, or Talend to automate and streamline these processes, ensuring data consistency and accuracy.

Database Management:

Choose a suitable database management system (DBMS) to store and organize your data. Relational databases like MySQL or PostgreSQL offer structured storage, while NoSQL databases like MongoDB or Cassandra excel at handling unstructured and semi-structured data. Evaluate the trade-offs between consistency, scalability, and ease of use when making your selection.

Data Warehousing:

Implementing a data warehouse empowers you to centralize and integrate data from multiple sources. Tools such as Amazon Redshift, Google BigQuery, or Snowflake enable efficient querying and analysis across vast datasets. Designing a well-structured data schema and optimizing queries can significantly enhance performance.

Data Exploration and Visualization:

Unleash the power of data exploration and visualization tools to unearth meaningful insights. Utilize platforms such as Tableau, Power BI, or Looker to create interactive and visually appealing dashboards. Leverage their drag-and-drop interfaces and extensive library of charts and graphs to communicate complex information effectively.

Statistical Analysis and Modeling:

Incorporate statistical analysis and modeling techniques into your environment to extract deeper insights. Utilize programming languages like Python or R along with libraries such as NumPy, Pandas, or scikit-learn to conduct exploratory data analysis, hypothesis testing, and build predictive models. Embrace the power of machine learning to uncover patterns and make accurate predictions.

Data Governance and Security:

Ensure data governance and security measures are in place to protect sensitive information and comply with regulations. Establish proper access controls, data masking, encryption, and backup procedures. Regularly audit your environment to identify vulnerabilities and address potential risks proactively.

Continuous Improvement and Learning:

Data analytics is an ever-evolving field, and fostering a culture of continuous improvement and learning is vital. Stay up to date with emerging technologies, attend conferences, join online communities, and encourage knowledge sharing within your team. Embrace agile methodologies to adapt quickly to changing business needs.

Setting up your data analytics environment is an exhilarating endeavor. With a clear vision, the right infrastructure, and the tools to extract insights, you'll unlock the true potential of your data. Embrace the journey, as it's a gateway to informed decision-making, strategic growth, and a competitive edge in today's data-driven world

Chapter Three: Collecting and Preparing Data

Packing for the adventure

Greetings from the intriguing realm of data analytics, where every piece of information has the potential to lead to a major finding. The vital first step in your quest to discover insightful information is gathering and preparing data. We'll delve into various aspects of collecting data and preparation in this page, stressing their significance and giving you in-depth, insightful, enthusiastic, and intriguing insights.

Consider starting a project to study consumer behavior at an online retailer. Finding patterns, preferences, and trends that can improve marketing strategies and the customer experience as a whole is your aim. Let's start our trip with comprehending the art of data collection.

Gathering Information: The Search Begins

Your data sources' quality, relevance, and diversity are critical to the success of your data analytics project. You should take into account a variety of data collection options to get the process started:

Internal Data Sources:

Begin by looking into the several data sources that exist within your company. A wealth of insightful information can be found in transactional data, customer databases, website logs, and customer support records. Explore these databases to find pertinent data that can help you with your business questions.

Exploring external data sources:

This will help you broaden your perspective. These could include data from social media, public data sources, market research papers, or data suppliers that specialize in a certain business. Finding these outside sources can give more background and improve your analysis.

Designing Surveys or Questionnaires:

Ask your target audience for a specific piece of information. To gather insightful qualitative and quantitative data, create well-thought-out questions. This approach can be aided by programs like SurveyMonkey and Google Forms.

Web scraping:

If you need information from websites or other online platforms, this technique can be very effective. You may extract structured data from web pages using programs like Python's BeautifulSoup or Scrapy, allowing you to collect important data like customer feedback or competition pricing.

Internet of Things (IoT):

IoT devices produce a lot of real-time data in several businesses. For instance, sensors on machinery can gather performance and efficiency data in the manufacturing industry. Recognize the value of this data stream in terms of operational advancements and preventive maintenance.

Partnerships and Collaborations:

Take into account establishing partnerships or working together with other businesses in your sector. This may offer up options for benchmarking, access to complementary data sets, and shared data resources, all of which can enhance your study.

Let's focus on the equally crucial process of data preparation now that we have started our treasure search and amassed a ton of data.

Preparing Data: The Secret to Unlocking Insights

In its unprocessed state, data might be disorganized, unreliable, and full of flaws. Data transformation and cleansing are required to make the acquired data appropriate for analysis. Let's examine the fundamental procedures for data preparation:

Data cleaning:

Check your data first for mistakes, missing numbers, duplicates, and outliers. To locate and fix these problems, use Excel, Python's Pandas, or R's dplyr. To maintain the integrity of your data, add missing values, eliminate duplicates, and treat outliers correctly.

Data fusion:

Combine data from several sources to produce a cohesive and complete data collection. Merge various data formats, align data pieces, and fix discrepancies. This phase is essential for developing a comprehensive understanding of your analytical subject.

For accurate analysis, data must frequently be translated into a standard format or scale. To ensure fair comparisons, normalize numerical data, convert units, and standardize variables. When necessary, use mathematical or statistical adjustments to fulfill the demands of your analysis.

Create new features or variables from existing data to improve your analysis by using feature engineering. Construct time-based features, compute ratios, or extract pertinent information from text. You can discover hidden links and patterns through feature engineering that might otherwise go unnoticed.

Dimensionality reduction approaches, like as Principal Component research (PCA) or feature selection algorithms, can assist make your research simpler when your data contains a lot of variables. The focus on the most important variables can be increased while computing efficiency is improved by reducing dimensionality.

Organize your data in a format that will allow for analysis. Ensure uniform data types, standardized date formats, and structured data organization. This phase streamlines the analysis that comes after and makes it simple to interpret the findings.

Data sample:

To reduce processing needs and expedite analysis, take into account sample strategies for huge data sets. The integrity of your study can be preserved while creating representative subgroups using random sampling, stratified sampling, or systematic sampling.

Documentation:

Keep complete records of every step of the data preparation process. Keep track of the actions completed, judgments made, and modifications made. When reproducing or sharing your analysis with coworkers or stakeholders, this documentation is crucial.

The Journey Goes On

As we come to an end with our study of gathering and preparing data for data analytics, keep in mind that this is only the start of your thrilling trip. Your upcoming ideas have the power to influence plans, spur innovation, and transform entire sectors.

Consider the craft of data gathering, relentlessly seek for various, pertinent sources, and follow your interest. Transform unstructured chaos into organized harmony while preparing data to ensure accuracy and consistency.

You are now prepared to begin the next step of your data analytics adventure—exploring, analyzing, and revealing the mysteries hidden within—with your treasure trove of painstakingly gathered and prepared data.

Unleashing the Power of Data: Data Quality and Data Cleaning

We're excited to continue our fascinating trip into the world of data analytics. We'll examine the critical facets of data quality and data cleaning in this chapter. By making sure your datasets are correct, trustworthy, and prepared for analysis, you and other aspiring data analysts are about to unleash the enormous potential buried inside them. So take out your magnifying lens and let's begin!

The Value of High-Quality Data

Consider attempting to construct a house on an unstable foundation. The same goes for attempting to derive useful insights from incorrect or insufficient data.

Data correctness, completeness, and consistency are all aspects of data quality that make sure it is suitable for its intended use. Any effective data analytics project is built on it. Decision-makers may trust analytical results when data quality is strong, which enables them to take assured, data-driven actions. Poor data quality, on the other hand, might introduce bias, inaccuracies, and false information, endangering the entire analytical process. As a result, any aspiring data analyst should make assuring data quality a primary priority.

Data Cleaning

Being a detective in the field of data analytics is similar to data cleansing. It is your responsibility to find and fix any mistakes, discrepancies, and abnormalities that may exist in your datasets. To make sure that your data is trustworthy, consistent, and prepared to expose its secrets, this process entails a number of investigative stages.

Finding Dirty Data is the First Step:

Finding dirty data is the first step. This may consist of inconsistent data, outliers, duplicate entries, and missing values. In order to find possible problems, you'll frequently need to study your data using various statistical approaches, visualization tools, and domain knowledge.

Handle Missing Values:

In real-world datasets, missing data is a frequent problem. You must make a decision on how to address these gaps without jeopardizing the validity of your research. Rows with missing data can be removed, values can be imputed using statistical approaches, or more sophisticated methods like machine learning algorithms can be used.

Identify and Eliminate Duplicates:

Duplicate records can bias your analysis and produce false results. Making ensuring that each observation in your dataset represents a distinct entity by locating and eliminating duplicates. Potential duplicates can be found and merged or removed using sophisticated algorithms and data matching techniques.

Outliers are data points that dramatically depart from the average; deal with them. These could be inaccurate entries or truly extreme figures. To prevent biased analysis, outliers must be found and handled properly. Your partners in this effort are solid statistical techniques, visual inspection, and domain expertise.

Data should be transformed and standardized since inconsistent data formats can be confusing and impair analysis. Your datasets' quality and comparability can be improved by standardizing units, normalizing variables, and converting data into a uniform format. No matter where the data came from, this phase makes sure it is ready for analysis.

Tools of the Trade

Data cleaning might be a time-consuming operation, but do not worry! There are numerous programs and tools available to help you with your quest for data quality. Let's examine a couple well-liked choices:

OpenRefine:

An open-source program for data cleaning and transformation, OpenRefine. For tasks like data parsing, grouping, and data augmentation, it offers a simple user interface. OpenRefine is a potent ally in your data cleaning endeavors because it permits the execution of customized scripts.

Trifacta Wrangler:

For non-technical users, Trifacta Wrangler is a user-friendly data cleaning tool. It uses machine learning algorithms to automate several data cleaning operations, which saves time and speeds up the procedure. Even novices may quickly clean and prepare their data for analysis using Trifacta Wrangler.

Python libraries:

Python is a flexible programming language that provides a number of libraries designed specifically for data cleaning, including pandas and NumPy. These libraries offer a vast selection of techniques and functions to deal with missing values, outliers, duplicates, and other issues. You may create a strong toolbox for data cleaning and analysis using Python in conjunction with well-known data science packages like scikit-learn and TensorFlow.

Data quality and cleaning are continual procedures rather than one-time tasks. Throughout your career, dealing with data will present you with fresh difficulties and complications. Every dataset will have its own distinct oddities and peculiarities, necessitating close observation and investigative work.Adopt the mindset of a data sleuth, constantly looking for the truth concealed in your datasets. You can distinguish yourself as a skilled data analyst by continually improving your data cleaning abilities and keeping up with the most recent methods and tools.

Congratulations! You've come a long way in realizing how important data quality and data cleaning are in the field of data analytics. Making sure your datasets are precise, dependable, and prepared for analysis paves the road for insightful conclusions and significant decision-making. Keep in mind that cleansing data is an adventure and a riddle that needs to be solved. Accept the challenge, pay attention, and let your passion motivate you. One clean dataset at a time, you can take on the data analytics world!

Continue to purge, analyze, and unleash the power of data!

Chapter Four: Exploratory Data Analysis

Opening up the bowels of insight

Excited to welcome you to Chapter 4 of our thrilling tour through the intriguing world of data analytics! We set off on an interesting journey known as exploratory data analysis (EDA) in this chapter. Imagine yourself as an inquisitive explorer exploring the depths of your data to find its patterns, insights, and mysteries while armed with a magnifying glass. EDA is your key to really comprehending your data, revealing its untold tales, and opening the door to additional research. So, grab your explorer's hat and let's embark on this enlightening expedition together!

Understanding the data we work with requires more than just running complicated algorithms and crunching figures. The compass that leads us across this vast and complex landscape is exploratory data analysis. It enables us to establish a link with every data point, get to know our data very well, and gain a thorough grasp of its traits and behaviors.

EDA is an evolving, dynamic process. It involves a dance between our curiosity and the information, a conversation between our inquiries and the conclusions that develop. It involves posing the appropriate queries, paying attention to the data's indications, and modifying our analysis as fresh information comes to light. Imagine EDA as a conversation with your dataset in which you listen intently to what it has to say and then react with ever-deeper questions to fully understand its meaning.

Exploratory data analysis is fundamentally a quest for knowledge. Armed with visualizations, statistical methods, and subject expertise, we explore unexplored territory. We explore the huge ocean of data through the lens of EDA, tracing its topography, spotting its peaks and valleys, and discovering the gems that lie therein.

EDA's fundamental objective is to draw insightful conclusions and patterns from data. We use a variety of tools and approaches to visualize and summarize our data, which helps us understand the distribution and overall structure of the data. As we go further into our datasets, histograms, scatter plots, box plots, and summary statistics become our dependable allies.

EDA also gives us the ability to spot abnormalities, outliers, and discrepancies that can compromise the validity of our analysis. We build an instinctive sense of what is typical and what is strange by immersing ourselves in the facts. These outliers frequently contain important data that might help us come up with fresh ideas or identify problems with the quality of the data that need more research.

Additionally, exploratory data analysis is vital in determining how we will model data and test hypotheses in the future. It assists us in locating pertinent factors, evaluating their relationships, and selecting the most effective ways. EDA offers the basis on which we build our analytical frameworks, ensuring the strength and depth of our following investigations.

We will begin a thorough investigation of EDA methods and best practices in this chapter. We will learn how to summarize and explain our data using statistical measures, how to depict data using a variety of graphs and charts, and how to find links and correlations that might help us make decisions. As we realize the full power of our data, get ready to immerse yourself in a world of visualizations, distributions, and insights.

So prepare your analytical talents, don your adventurer's cap, and embark with us on this thrilling journey into the core of exploratory data analysis. Let's set out on a mission to unearth the unseen tales, patterns, and insights that our data conceals!

Data Visualization and Descriptive Statistics: Uncovering the Beauty of Numbers

Descriptive statistics and data visualization act as our dependable guides in the enormous field of data analysis, shedding light on our datasets' hidden patterns and insights. We use these potent tools to turn raw data into a colorful picture that tells a fascinating tale, just like an artist might with a paintbrush. Let's explore descriptive statistics and data visualization to see how they accurately, clearly, and enthusiastically bring our data to life!

In the world of data, descriptive statistics are the storytellers. They enable us to succinctly and meaningfully summarize and describe the essential elements of our dataset. These statistics give us a broad overview of the landscape of our data, capturing its central tendency, variability, and distribution.

Consider a dataset that includes a collection of people's heights. The mean, or average height, can be found using descriptive statistics, which provides a measure of central tendency. Additionally, the standard deviation reveals how far the heights depart from the mean and sheds light on the degree of data variability. With the help of descriptive statistics, we can quickly and easily identify the main points of our data and its general distribution.

However, a number alone might be sterile and esoteric. Data visualization can help by giving our data life and transforming it into a dynamic tapestry of colors, shapes, and patterns. Rows and columns of numbers are converted into engaging images through the use of expertly produced visual representations, enabling a better understanding.

We may examine our data via data visualization, which stimulates our senses and makes use of our natural visual cognition. We can use the capacity of visual perception to discover patterns, trends, and relationships that might otherwise go undetected by making graphs, charts, and plots.

Picture a histogram, where each bar represents a range of heights, and you are graphing the heights of our group of people. This representation not only shows how the heights are distributed, but it also enables us to see any peaks, gaps, or clusters that might contain important information. The link between height and other factors, such as weight or age, can also be examined using scatter plots, which may identify potential correlations or outliers.

We may study our data from a variety of views and angles thanks to the dynamic and interactive nature of some visualizations. To better comprehend our data, we can zoom in, filter, or overlay several visualizations with a few clicks. We may access new levels of understanding thanks to these interactive capabilities, which facilitate the development of hypotheses and data-driven decision-making.

Additionally, data visualization is not just for numerical data. Additionally, it can shed light on categorical data using bar charts, pie charts, or stacked charts, enabling us to comprehend the make-up, distribution, and proportions of various categories within our information. Data visualization offers a potent lens through which we may investigate and express the stories within our data, whether it's showing consumer demographics, product sales by area, or sentiment analysis of social media data.

So, when you go out on your data analysis adventure equipped with descriptive statistics and data visualization, let your imagination soar. Accept the challenge of transforming data into fascinating visual stories, and release the data's potential to enlighten, inspire, and transform.

Always keep in mind that descriptive statistics and data visualization aren't simply tools; they're also creative outlets that let us speak intelligibly to data. Enter the world of descriptive statistics and data visualization, then let your data speak volumes through its vivid, perceptive, and enthusiastic representation.

Identifying Data and Unraveling Trends: Illuminating Insights in Data Analysis

Finding useful data and seeing patterns and trends are like having superpowers in the fascinating world of data analysis. When the jigsaw pieces start fitting together, a better picture of the world concealed in the data emerges. So let's dive into the thrilling process of locating data and detecting trends, and then watch with accuracy, zeal, and a dash of wonder as the magic of data analysis plays out before our very eyes!

In its unprocessed state, data can be confusing and overwhelming. It feels like we are at a crowded bazaar where there are many vendors shouting for our attention.

The secret is in our capacity to distinguish the appropriate vendors—the pertinent data points—among the noise. To choose the data that supports our analysis objectives and shines light on the questions we are trying to answer, we must be diligent and discerning.

Consider that you are investigating consumer purchase information for an online store. Insights that can inform marketing strategy are what you're looking for. You carefully pinpoint pertinent elements as you delve into the data, such as consumer demographics, purchasing history, and product categories. By choosing the appropriate data, you create the conditions for revealing insightful information about each variable, which each holds a tale and a piece of the puzzle.

Once the data has been located, the exciting task of uncovering trends and patterns may begin. Imagine yourself as a detective searching meticulously through the data for hints that could lead you to important discoveries while equipped with statistical methods and visualization tools.

Regression analysis is one statistical technique that can reveal correlations between variables, allowing you to identify trends and make predictions. For instance, if you examine the relationship between advertising spending and sales, you can find a positive correlation showing that higher sales are caused by increased advertising investment.

Data visualization is essential for spotting trends as well. Line graphs can demonstrate how a variable, like website traffic or customer satisfaction levels, has increased or decreased over time. Heatmaps can indicate trends in categorical data, such as the most popular product categories or the busiest times of day for customers. By bringing the data to life through visualizations, we can see trends and patterns that could be hidden in rows and columns of numbers.

Keep in mind that understanding the context of trends is an important part of data analysis. Context is crucial. To obtain a comprehensive grasp of the trends you find, go deep into the data, investigate its subtleties, and combine your analytical abilities with subject expertise. Do sales follow a seasonal pattern? Do demographic variables affect consumer preferences? Your decisions, tactics, and company outcomes will be influenced by the trends you derive insights from.

So, when you embark on your data analysis journey, embrace the excitement of discovering data and uncovering trends. Be observant, thorough, and eager as you look for the treasures concealed in your dataset. Keep in mind that data analysis is an art of interpretation where you must uncover the tales the data is trying to tell you and turn them into useful information.

Allow your superpower of data identification and trend analysis to lead you to a world of fascinating discoveries and game-changing choices. Accept the data-driven journey that lies ahead and watch as the beauty of data analysis comes to life!

Embracing Imperfections: Taming Missing Values and Outliers in Data Analysis

We frequently face incomplete datasets rife with missing values and outliers in the large field of data analysis. Fear not, however, for these flaws give us excellent chances to showcase our analytical skills and discover deeper insights. So let's go out on an exhilarating trip to handle missing values and outliers while armed with accuracy, zeal, and a never-ending drive to find the truth in our data.

Missing values are comparable to misplaced jigsaw puzzle pieces. They interfere with our dataset's completeness, which could result in biased analysis and incorrect results. But don't worry, we can address these elusive gaps in our data using a variety of strategies that are at our disposal.

We must first recognize the missing values and comprehend their patterns. Are they systematically happening or distributed at random? We can see the extent and distribution of missingness by graphically representing missing data patterns, such as through heatmaps or bar charts.

We then use methods to deal with missing values. Imputation is a popular strategy in which missing values are replaced with approximated values derived from the available data. For instance, we might use the mean or median age of the available data to impute missing age values in a dataset. We can minimize the effect of missingness on our analysis while still maintaining the integrity of our dataset using imputation.

However, since imputing values adds assumptions and inherent biases, we must proceed with caution. For our particular analysis objectives, it is critical to take into account the type of missingness and the implications of imputation. Sensitivity analysis, in which we evaluate the resistance of our results to various imputation techniques, should always be conducted in conjunction with imputation.

Let's now focus on outliers, the rebels inside our data that challenge the norm. Outliers can have a significant impact, skewing statistical metrics and producing false conclusions. They push us to look farther, to comprehend the underlying factors and possible importance.

Statistical methods and a watchful eye are needed to spot outliers. Outliers can be found and seen using powerful tools like box plots, scatter plots, and z-scores. We can spot extreme numbers that differ greatly from the majority of the data by looking at these graphic representations.

But this is where things become interesting. Outliers, which indicate particular phenomena or extraordinary circumstances, can provide insightful information. They might provide insight into atypical client behavior, extraordinary performance, or problems with data quality. We must evaluate the significance and effect of outliers on our work as data analysts. Do the data points indeed represent unusual occurrences, or do they instead point to measurement or data entry errors? We can decide how to handle outliers in our analysis by comprehending the situation and looking into potential causes.

In data analysis, handling missing values and outliers is not merely a technicality. We may hone our analytical abilities, unearth hidden stories, and improve our comprehension of the data. Therefore, accept the flaws because they open up new perspectives. Consider every missing value and outlier as a riddle that needs to be solved, and allow your curiosity lead you to the answers hiding in your data.

Chapter Five: Manipulation and Transformation of Data

Building Data the awesome way

Welcome to the next exciting part of our fascinating journey into the fascinating world of data analytics! The alchemical procedures that enable us to shape, mold, and refine our data into a potent resource for analysis are the subject of this chapter, which delves into the art of data manipulation and transformation. Consider data manipulation and transformation as the weapons in our toolbox that we may use to create order out of chaos and maximize the value of our data. Roll up your sleeves and get ready to set off on a revolutionary adventure that will enable you to harness the power of data with accuracy, insight, and unbridled joy!

Our hidden weapon is our capacity to manipulate data to mold, restructure, and reorganize it to meet our analytical demands. It's comparable to a skilled chef putting together the perfect combination of components to make a mouthwatering dish. We can filter away pointless data, combine and link databases, add new variables, and aggregate data at various granularities using data manipulation. We have the ability to sculpt our data into a form that best reveals the insights we seek, molding it to match the shapes of our research.

Our chisel, which allows us to shape our data into a more appealing shape, is data transformation. It's comparable to an artist using instinct and ingenuity to add color and life to a white canvas. We can apply mathematical functions, normalize variables, standardize units of measurement, and produce derived variables through data transformation. We are allowed to change our data in ways that improve its quality, make analysis easier, and lead to a deeper understanding.

Data translation and manipulation enable us to understand the complexities of our data and reveal its untapped potential. These methods give us the freedom and control to unlock the full potential of our data, whether we're working with unclean, raw data from many sources or preparing it for a particular analysis method.

We start a thorough exploration of data modification and transformation techniques in this chapter. We will gain knowledge of effective programming languages and tools for filtering, sorting, and reshaping our data. We'll learn the fine art of handling outliers, missing numbers, and data purification. We will also explore how data standardization, scaling, and feature engineering may be revolutionary. As we go into the world of data modification and transformation, get prepared to unleash the potential of your data.

So let's start this transformational adventure together and grab our toolbox of data manipulation and transformation strategies. We get a little bit closer to realizing the full potential of our data with each line of code and transformation operation. As we delve farther into the world of data analytics, get ready to mold your data and give it life.

Data Filtering and Selection: Revealing Insights with Care

Filtering and choosing data is one of the core activities in the broad world of data analytics. Consider it as sorting through a hoard of riches to find the gold nuggets among the pebbles. We can zoom in on the precise information we need, find unnoticed trends, and gain insightful knowledge by filtering and selecting data. We'll examine the art and science of data selection and filtering in this section, giving you the ability to navigate big datasets with accuracy and grace.

Data filtering is similar to separating sand grains from bigger particles using a fine-mesh sieve. We can focus more narrowly by removing data sets that satisfy certain requirements. By using filters, we eliminate extraneous data and are left with only the jewels that are important to the objectives of our investigation.

Depending on the nature of our data and the precise criteria we wish to use, we have access to a number of filtering approaches. Using conditional expressions to filter data based on logical conditions is one frequent method. For instance, we can filter sales data to only include transactions done within a certain time window or by a particular client segment.

Using query languages like SQL (Structured Query Language) is another effective method for filtering data. By utilizing its robust syntax and operators, SQL offers an organized and effective method for filtering data based on complicated conditions. We may create SQL queries that extract data from databases depending on a variety of parameters, allowing us to focus in on the precise data we need.

Filtering and data selection go hand in hand. We can choose particular columns or variables that are pertinent to our research after utilizing filters to reduce the size of our dataset. By removing the noise and clutter from our data, this technique aids in our ability to concentrate on its most important elements.

It's crucial to take into account the dimensions and features that correspond with the goals of our study while choosing the data. Variables may be chosen depending on their applicability, importance, or type of data. We can focus on the essential characteristics and patterns that contain the answers to our analytical inquiries by choosing the appropriate variables.

Data Aggregation and Sorting: Discovering Patterns and Gaining Insights

Imagine a disorganized mass of jigsaw pieces without any discernible organization. Sorting and combining data is similar to putting those jigsaw pieces in order, creating patterns that let us see the greater image. By categorizing and summarizing data, identifying trends, and exposing insights that might otherwise go unnoticed, these strategies help us understand our data better.

When sorting data, rows or observations are put in a certain order based on one or more variables. Sorting gives our data structure and makes it easier for us to spot patterns and trends. For instance, we could order client data by how frequently they make purchases, starting with the most frequent consumers and working our way down. With the help of this arrangement, we may identify devoted customers, recurring buying behaviors, and potentially adjust marketing efforts accordingly.

The process of summarizing information into groups or categories and presenting it at a higher level is known as data aggregation. We can reduce complicated datasets to more manageable and insightful representations with the use of aggregation. We can, for example, combine sales data by month to determine monthly revenue, spot seasonal trends, and evaluate overall performance over time. Summaries, averages, counts, minimum and maximum values, as well as the creation of unique metrics depending on particular business needs, are all examples of common aggregation procedures. Large amounts of data can be condensed through aggregation, allowing us to concentrate on important indicators and comprehend the broad trends and patterns that emerge.

Since grouping involves dividing data into groupings based on shared traits, it is strongly related to aggregation. By grouping data, we can examine it at various granularities and find insights within particular categories or sectors. For instance, to better understand the differences and similarities between different client segments, we can organize consumer data according to demographic factors like age or region.

Using strong methods like sorting, aggregating, and grouping, we may reveal the underlying structure of our data. They give us the framework and structure we need to spot trends, make comparisons, and draw conclusions from our investigation. We can produce attractive visual representations of our data that highlight trends and assist data-driven storytelling by combining these strategies with visualization tools.

Data Transformation Techniques: Harnessing Your Data's Full Potential

Similar to shaping clay, data transformation enables us to change our data to realize its full potential. With the use of these strategies, we can create, scale, normalize, and standardize our data, thereby raising its quality, analyzing results, and providing deeper insights. This section will examine several data transformation methods and the applications for them, giving you the knowledge and abilities to change your data into useful analytical assets.

A typical technique is normalization, which rescales data to a standard scale and removes any inherent biases brought on by varying units or scales. The process of normalization makes sure that variables with various measurement ranges have an equivalent impact on the study. The min-max scaling, a well-liked normalization method, maps data to a particular range, often between 0 and 1. This method converts the data points into a standardized scale while maintaining the relative relationships between them.

Another data transformation method that aims to produce a common mean and standard deviation for variables is standardization. The data are changed to have a mean value of 0 and a standard deviation value of 1. When working with variables that have various distributions and measuring units, standardization is especially helpful. We may directly compare the variables and find patterns that may not be there in the raw data.

Data having skewed distributions can be scaled using techniques like log transformation or power transformation to make them more symmetrical and regularly distributed. When working with severely skewed data, log transformation is frequently utilized since it shrinks large values and expands tiny values, creating a distribution that is more evenly distributed. Power transformations that reduce skewness and bring data closer to a normal distribution include square root and cube root transformations.

In order to increase the predictive ability of our models, feature engineering is a creative and adaptable data transformation strategy that entails the creation of new variables or the modification of existing ones. Combining variables, coming up with new terminology for interactions, or drawing out pertinent data from already-existing variables are all examples of feature engineering. For instance, to measure the level of customer unhappiness in a customer churn analysis, we might create a new variable that represents the proportion of customer complaints to the total number of transactions.

Data transformation strategies help our analytical models run more efficiently while also enhancing the quality and usability of our data. Our data can be transformed to reveal hidden links, increase model precision, and provide a greater understanding of underlying patterns and trends.

Conclusively, data transformation methods, sorting and aggregation methods, and filtering and selection methods all play crucial roles in the data analytics process. They give us the ability to search through huge datasets, concentrate on the most important facts, find patterns, and derive insightful conclusions. By mastering these techniques, you'll acquire the power to transform raw data into actionable knowledge, equipping yourself with the tools to make informed decisions and drive meaningful outcomes.

Chapter Five: Statistical Analysis

The Magic of Numbers and Patterns

Welcome to the fascinating world of statistics! We set out on a journey of discovery in this chapter as we investigate the fundamental ideas of statistics, including hypothesis testing, confidence intervals, correlation, and regression analysis. Making educated judgments, spotting trends, and developing a deeper understanding of the world around us are all made possible by statistical analysis, which is like a key that unlocks the insights that are hidden in our data. So buckle up and prepare to explore the wonderful world of statistical analysis!

Basic Statistical Concepts: Building Blocks of Data Understanding

It's important to become familiar with the fundamental ideas that form the basis of statistical analysis before we go into its depths. The entire purpose of statistics is to summarize and evaluate data in order to make meaningful judgments. Descriptive statistics, which enable us to enumerate and explain the key features of our data, are where we start. We may better comprehend the central tendency, spread, and shape of our data distribution by using metrics like mean, median, mode, variance, and standard deviation.

Another key idea in statistics is **probability**. It offers a framework for estimating uncertainty and comprehending the probability of occurrences taking place. The capacity to compute the probabilies of alternative possibilities makes probability theory an essential tool for making decisions in uncertain situations.

Sampling is an essential technique in statistics that enables us to generalize findings from a smaller subset of data, known as a sample, to a larger population. Even when only a small portion of the data is examined, we can reliably derive conclusions about the population by using the right sampling techniques.

The foundation of statistical analysis is **inferential statistics**, which let us infer, draw conclusions, and test hypotheses about a population based on sample data. We can determine the statistical significance of associations, calculate population parameters, and make predictions using inferential statistics.

Hypothesis Testing and Confidence Intervals: Uncovering the Truth

A useful tool for assessing the veracity of assertions or hypotheses about a population based on sample data is hypothesis testing. Making a null hypothesis, which denotes the status quo or the absence of an effect, and an alternative hypothesis, which implies a connection or effect, is required.

We use statistical tests that give evidence against the null hypothesis to examine hypotheses. These tests determine a test statistic, like the t-statistic or z-score, that quantifies the discrepancy between our sample data and what the null hypothesis predicts. We decide if the data support rejecting the null hypothesis in favor of the alternative hypothesis by comparing the test statistic to a crucial value or computing the p-value.

Based on sample data, confidence intervals offer a way to calculate population metrics like the mean or proportion. A confidence interval is a set of values that, with a high degree of certainty, encompass the true population parameter. For instance, a population's mean weight's 95% confidence interval can fall between 60kg and 70kg. The precision of our estimate is reflected in the breadth of the gap, with smaller intervals offering more accurate estimations.

Correlation and Regression Analysis: Unveiling Relationships and Making Predictions

We can investigate links between variables and create predictions based on these relationships using correlation and regression analysis. The strength and direction of the linear link between two variables are measured by correlation. It enables us to comprehend the relationship between changes in one variable and those in another. The Pearson's correlation coefficient, for example, has a range of -1 to 1, with values close to -1 suggesting a strong negative association, close to 1 indicating a strong positive relationship, and close to 0 indicating no significant relationship.

By creating a mathematical model to forecast the value of one variable based on the values of other variables, regression analysis advances correlation. While multiple linear regression takes into account more than two variables, simple linear regression entails modeling the relationship between two variables using a straight line. We can anticipate the result variable, evaluate the relevance of the predictors, and comprehend how changes in the predictors affect it using regression analysis.

We can evaluate the goodness of fit of our model and discover outliers and significant observations with the use of regression analysis. We may assess the robustness and relevance of our regression model by analyzing metrics like R-squared, modified R-squared, and p-values of coefficients.

The foundation of statistical analysis is made up of these statistical ideas: fundamental statistics, hypothesis testing, confidence intervals, correlation, and regression analysis. We can gain important insights, facilitate decision-making, and stimulate creativity by utilizing their power. We have the tools to examine the underlying patterns in our data, make reliable predictions, and learn more about the world around us thanks to statistical analysis.

In order to fully appreciate the power of data analysis, let's set off on this statistical trip together. Every time a statistical test is run, a confidence interval is generated, or a correlation is investigated, new information is learned, presumptions are questioned, and data-driven discoveries are made that change how we perceive the world.

Chapter Six: Predictive Analytics

Asking the great stones

Greetings from the fascinating world of predictive analysis! We set out on a trip in this chapter that takes us beyond comprehending historical facts and into the world of making predictions about the future. Making precise forecasts, seeing patterns, and gaining a competitive edge are all made possible through predictive analysis, which is like looking into a crystal ball. So buckle up and prepare to delve into the fascinating world of predictive analysis!

The capacity to forecast future events is a game-changer in a world that is changing quickly and is driven by data. Organizations may anticipate customer behavior, improve operations, reduce risks, and reach well-informed decisions thanks to predictive analysis. Predictive analysis gives us a view into the future by utilizing historical data, statistical models, machine learning algorithms, and sophisticated analytics approaches. This insight enables us to plan, prepare, and succeed in an uncertain future.

Predictive analysis, at its foundation, entails identifying significant patterns and relationships in historical data in order to create models that are capable of making precise predictions. We can learn important lessons from the past that help us comprehend the future. Predictive models use correlations, patterns, and trends found in historical data to make predictions about the future based on fresh data inputs.

Unleashing the Power of Future Insights with Predictive Modeling

Based on previous data, predictive modeling is a potent tool that enables us to generate precise predictions and foresee future outcomes. It makes use of statistical algorithms, machine learning methods, and advanced analytics to sift through the data and find patterns, relationships, and trends that help us foresee the future. We will go into the foundational ideas and elements of predictive modeling in this section, giving you the tools you need to maximize its potential and uncover insightful data.

The Predictive Modeling Idea

Predictive modeling is fundamentally the process of creating mathematical models that can learn from historical data and predict or forecast upcoming events or outcomes. It investigates the link between the target variable—the variable we want to predict—and a group of predictor variables, also referred to as features. The model may generate predictions on fresh, unforeseen data by learning the patterns and relationships within the data through training on historical data.

Numerous sectors use predictive modeling in a variety of ways. It can be employed to optimize marketing efforts, forecast revenue, predict customer churn, estimate product demand, and much more. Predictive modeling's strength resides in its capacity to offer insightful guidance and influence decision-making.

What Makes Up Predictive Modeling

Let's examine predictive modeling's essential elements to gain a better understanding of it:

Training Data:

Historical data are used to train predictive models. A set of observations with known values for the predictor variables and the target variable make up the training data. It provides the framework for the model to discover the underlying correlations and patterns in the data.

Predictor Factors:

These independent factors are thought to have a significant impact on forecasting the target variable. They could be numerical, category, or a mix of the two. A crucial stage in predictive modeling is the selection of pertinent predictor variables because it directly affects the model's predicted accuracy.

Target Variable:

The target variable, sometimes referred to as the dependent variable, is the variable we wish to forecast. Indicators might be categorical (such as customer attrition) or continuous (such as sales revenue). The best predictive modeling approach will depend on the characteristics of the target variable.

Model Construction:

The construction of a predictive model entails choosing the best modeling approach, training the model with training data, and refining its parameters. Different modeling approaches, such as linear regression, logistic regression, decision trees, random forests, support vector machines, or neural networks, might be used, depending on the nature of the problem and the data.

Model Evaluation:

After the model has been trained, it must be examined to determine its effectiveness and dependability. The model's predictive ability can be assessed using metrics including accuracy, precision, recall, F1-score, and area under the curve (AUC). Cross-validation is one method for estimating a model's performance on unknown data while preventing overfitting.

Model Deployment:

Once the model has been assessed and shown to be satisfactory, it can be put into use to create forecasts based on brand-new, unforeseen data. In order to guarantee scalability and real-time prediction capabilities, this entails integrating the model with already-in place systems or workflows.

Factors to Take into Account for Predictive Modeling

To ensure its success, predictive modeling may provide a number of issues and obstacles that must be taken into account. A few of these are:

Data Quality:

The performance of the prediction model is greatly influenced by the caliber of the training data. To prevent making biased or incorrect predictions, it is crucial to have data that is clear, trustworthy, and representative. To improve data quality, data preprocessing methods like data cleansing, addressing missing information, and dealing with outliers are frequently used.

Feature Selection and Engineering:

The predictive capacity of the model can be considerably impacted by choosing the appropriate set of predictor variables and developing new features. To find the most pertinent features for precise predictions, careful consideration of domain expertise, exploratory data analysis, and feature selection approaches is required.

Overfitting and Underfitting:

Overfitting is the process of a model becoming extremely complicated and capturing noise or random fluctuations in the training data, which results in poor generalization on unobserved data. On the other side, underfitting happens when the model is too straightforward to identify the underlying trends in the data. The complexity of the model must be balanced to prevent either overfitting or underfitting.

Complexity vs. Interpretability:

Some predictive modeling methods, like deep learning algorithms, can be very complex and challenging to understand. Although these models could have very good predicted accuracy, interpretability is frequently compromised. The trade-off between complexity and interpretability needs to be taken into account depending on the situation and requirements.

Continuous Learning and Adaptability:

In order to maintain their efficacy, predictive models need to be constantly reviewed and modified. The model might need to be retrained or calibrated to take into account changing patterns and trends when new data becomes available.

With the help of predictive modeling, we may fully utilize the potential of historical data and gain insightful knowledge about what will happen in the future. We may use predictive modeling to make precise forecasts, improve decision-making processes, and obtain a competitive advantage by comprehending its basic concepts, elements, and obstacles. This information will enable you to traverse the world of data-driven predictions and uncover the secrets of the future, whether you're a data scientist, business analyst, or hobbyist eager to explore the power of predictive modeling.

Building and Evaluating Predictive Models: Unleashing the Power of Data-driven Insights

Greetings from the fascinating realm of developing and analyzing predictive models! We will delve deeply into the process of creating precise and trustworthy models that can project future results based on historical data in this chapter. We can harness the power of data-driven insights and produce reliable forecasts by combining statistical algorithms, machine learning methods, and advanced analytics. So let's start this adventure and learn the essential procedures for creating and assessing predictive models.

The Foundation of Predictive Modeling

We need to identify the issue we're trying to tackle before we can start developing a predictive model. It is essential to comprehend the objective clearly and to identify the target variable we hope to predict. For instance, our goal variable would be whether a customer will leave us, if we wanted to anticipate customer turnover. The problem must be defined in order to choose the appropriate variables, modeling strategies, and evaluation criteria.

The Foundation of Predictive Models: Data Gathering and Preparation

We need high-quality data in order to create a prediction model. This entails compiling pertinent information from a range of sources, including transaction logs, client information, and demographic data. Data cleansing, addressing missing values, dealing with outliers, and translating variables into a suitable format are all essential components of data preparation. We build a solid foundation for precise predictions by ensuring data integrity and quality.

Engineering and Feature Selection: Harnessing the Power of Variables

For models to be effective, the proper set of features or variables with predictive potential must be chosen. Finding the factors that are most important to the prediction task is called feature selection. The selection of features can be helped by domain expertise, exploratory data analysis, and statistical techniques. To further improve the predictive power of our models, feature engineering enables us to alter, merge, or create new variables. This procedure calls for inventiveness and a thorough comprehension of the issue at hand.

Model Selection: Selecting the Appropriate Method for the Job

We now choose an acceptable modeling technique after the data has been prepared and the features have been chosen. The type of problem, the data, and the desired result all influence the model that is selected. It could include more sophisticated machine learning techniques like decision trees, random forests, support vector machines, or neural networks, as well as more conventional statistical models like linear regression and logistic regression. To choose the most appropriate model, considerable consideration is required as each technique has advantages and disadvantages.

Unleashing the Power of Learning Through Model Training and Parameter Optimization

We then train the chosen model with the collected data. The model adjusts its parameters to decrease errors and maximize predicted accuracy as it learns from the patterns and relationships found in the data. The model's parameters are iteratively adjusted during the training process, enabling the model to adapt and enhance its predictions over time. Finding the ideal balance between underfitting and overfitting is the key to training a model that generalizes well to new data.

Model Evaluation: Uncovering the Assessment's Power

It is essential to examine the predictive model's performance in order to determine its dependability and accuracy. Area under the curve (AUC) and F1-score are two evaluation metrics that offer important insights into the model's predicting ability. In order to prevent overfitting, methods like cross-validation measure the model's performance on hypothetical data. We can choose the best model to use moving forward by analyzing many models and contrasting their performance.

Model Deployment and Monitoring: Understanding Prediction's Power

It's time to put our predictive model into production after it's working well. This entails integrating the model into current workflows or systems to enable it to make predictions on fresh, unforeseen data. To make sure the model keeps making correct predictions, it is crucial to track its performance over time. The model may need to be retrained or recalibrated as new data becomes available in order to keep up with changing patterns and trends.

Predictive model development and evaluation is a potent process that enables us to fully utilize the potential of data-driven insights. We unlock the power of precise predictions by identifying the issue, gathering and preparing the data, choosing pertinent features, training the model, assessing its performance, and putting it into use. The ability to create and assess predictive models offers access to insightful insights and well-informed decision-making, regardless of your background as a data scientist, analyst, or hobbyist. So enjoy the adventure, investigate your options, and let the power of data guide your forecasts.

Classification and Regression Algorithms: Unveiling the Power of Predictive Analytics

Classification and regression algorithms are two essential methods that help us create precise predictions and derive insightful knowledge from data in the large subject of predictive analytics. These algorithms give us the means to address a wide range of issues, from identifying client segments to detecting fraud, forecasting housing prices, or even diagnosing diseases. We will examine the fundamental ideas, well-liked methods, and practical uses of classification and regression in this chapter, enabling you to fully realize the potential of predictive analytics.

Predicting categorical outcomes through classification

The art of classification involves identifying predetermined classes or categories for data instances or making predictions about categorical outcomes. Consider a scenario in which you wish to forecast a customer's likelihood of churning based on a dataset of customer information. The goal variable has two classifications in this standard binary classification problem: churn and non-churn. Classifying emails into spam, promotional, or personal categories is one example of a classification challenge. Other classification issues can also have several classes.

Let's examine a few well-known classification algorithms:

Logistic Regression:

Contrary to its name, logistic regression is a classification algorithm that estimates the likelihood that a given instance would fall into a certain class. A logistic function is used to model the connection between the predictor factors and the likelihood that an event will occur. The usage of logistic regression is widespread across many industries and is easy to understand.

Decision Trees:

Decision trees are flexible algorithms that create a tree-like model to base choices on the input information. Each leaf node corresponds to a class or outcome, while each internal node represents a feature. Both categorical and continuous data can be handled using decision trees, which are logical and simple to comprehend. CART (Classification and Regression Trees) and C4.5 are two common decision tree algorithms.

Random Forest Ensemble:

When making predictions, the Random Forest ensemble approach mixes several different decision trees. By including randomness in the tree-building process, for as by randomly choosing a subset of features and bootstrapping the training data, it produces a diverse collection of decision trees. In addition to offering feature significance values and being extremely accurate in many classification tasks, Random Forest is resilient against overfitting.

Support Vector Machines (SVM):

A potent algorithm, SVM finds the best hyperplane in a high-dimensional space to divide classes. In order to be resistant to noise and outliers, it seeks to maximize the margin between classes. SVM uses several kernel functions to address both linear and non-linear classification tasks.

Predicting Continuous Outcomes through Regression

On the other hand, regression focuses on forecasting continuous numerical results. In order to create precise predictions, it seeks to model the link between the independent factors and the target variable. An example of a typical regression problem is estimating housing values based on features like location, size, number of rooms, and other pertinent factors.

Let's look into a few well-known regression algorithms:

Linear Regression:

A linear equation is used in linear regression, a straightforward yet effective approach, to represent the connection between the independent variables and the target variable. The variables are assumed to have a linear connection, and the coefficients that minimize the sum of squared residuals are estimated. Due of its simplicity and ease of interpretation, linear regression is frequently utilized.

Decision Trees for Regression:

By estimating continuous values rather than classes at the leaf nodes, decision trees can also be utilized for regression applications. The predicted value for a given instance is the average value of the examples falling into the appropriate leaf node, and the tree structure is built based on the features. Decision trees can handle both categorical and continuous data and offer models that are easy to understand.

Random Forest:

Regression problems can also be solved using Random Forest, much like classification problems. Random Forest makes forecasts that are more precise and consistent by combining the results of several decision trees. It successfully manages interactions between features and captures non-linear relationships.

Gradient Boosting:

Gradient Boosting is an ensemble technique that combines decision trees, which are often weak predictive models, to produce a strong predictive model. Each model is developed gradually, with an emphasis on minimizing the mistakes caused by earlier models. Because of their excellent prediction accuracy and adaptability, gradient boosting algorithms like XGBoost and LightGBM are widely used.

Chapter Seven: Data Visualization

Telling the most beautiful stories

The fascinating world of data visualization is yours to explore. We will set out on a journey in this chapter that will turn unprocessed data into engrossing visual narratives. In order to convey complicated information in a way that is both visually appealing and accessible, data visualization is a skill that blends creativity, analytical thinking, and design principles. We can find patterns, trends, and insights that might be concealed in columns of data and tables by utilizing graphs, charts, interactive components, and maps. Let's explore the world of data visualization and see how effective visual storytelling is.

Importance of Data Visualization

We are surrounded by a great amount of information in today's data-driven society. Without good visualization, raw data can be overwhelming and difficult to understand. Data visualization helps us understand complex ideas, see trends, and make defensible decisions by serving as a link between the data and our understanding. It enables us to engage stakeholders, effectively communicate findings, and move meaningful actions based on data-driven proof.

The Rules for Successful Data Visualization

We must take into account a few fundamental ideas in order to produce powerful visualizations:

Clarity:

The visualization should be clear and concise in its delivery of the desired message. Make sure the information is presented logically and intuitively, and stay away from clutter and pointless distractions.

Accuracy:

It is essential to appropriately represent the facts and prevent information from being distorted or interpreted incorrectly. To portray the data honestly, pick appropriate scales, labels, and representations.

Relevance:

Concentrate on the data's most pertinent features and emphasize its most important conclusions. To keep the audience's interest and make it easier for them to swiftly understand the primary idea, eliminate noise and superfluous elements.

Context:

Give the data context by supplying pertinent background knowledge, justifications, or comparisons. This aids the audience in comprehending the importance of the findings and drawing pertinent conclusions.

Aesthetics:

Visual attractiveness is necessary to draw in and hold the attention of the spectator. Use design principles for layout, typography, and color to produce aesthetically pleasing visualizations.

Data visualization Forms

To effectively depict data, data visualization offers a wide range of methodologies and tools. A few examples of prevalent visualizations are:

Line Charts:

Line charts, for example, are used to show patterns and trends across time. They are very helpful for displaying alterations, variations, or correlations in data.

Bar Charts:

Comparing categorical data or displaying discrete values is best done with bar charts. They give comparisons and rankings a clear visual depiction.

Pie Charts:

Pie charts show the percentages and proportions of an entire. They are useful for comparing the relative sizes of categories or displaying portions of a larger whole.

Scatter Plots:

Scatter plots are useful for analyzing the relationship between two continuous variables. d. They aid in locating outliers, clusters, and correlations in the data.

Maps:

Maps show geographic information and patterns. They are fantastic at showcasing regional variances, spatial distributions, and place-based insights.

Visualization of Interactive Data

By enabling interactive data exploration, interactive data visualization elevates the viewing experience for the user. Users may dive down, filter, and change the visual representation, giving them the power to get more information and uncover relationships that were previously hidden. Interactive visualizations create meaningful interactions with the data, facilitate data discovery, and increase engagement.

Data visualization is an effective method for maximizing the value of data by turning it into interesting and insightful visual narratives. We may use it to identify patterns and trends, effectively explain complex information, and enhance decision-making processes. We can produce powerful visualizations that enthrall and educate audiences by adhering to the criteria of clarity, truth, relevance, context, and aesthetics. So embrace data visualization, make the most of its potential, and learn to tell stories with data like a pro.

Choosing the Right Visualization Techniques: A Guide to Effective Data Representation

A strong tool for simplifying complex data into understandable visual representations is data visualization. It can be difficult to choose the visualization style that is most appropriate for your data and the insights you want to share, though, because there are so many of them accessible. In this chapter, we'll examine the crucial criteria to take into account when selecting visualization techniques and offer advice to assist you in making judgments that will effectively convey your data-driven story.

Understand Your Data

Understanding the nature of your data is vital before choosing a visualization strategy. Think about the following elements:

Decide if your data are categorized or numerical in order to proceed. While numerical data comprises of quantifiable amounts, categorical data is separated into distinct groups or categories. Using this distinction as a guide, choose the best visualization techniques.

Data Distribution:

Examine how your data are distributed. Does it have any unusual patterns, is it normally distributed, or is it skewed? Different visualization methods are more appropriate to portray certain distribution types.

Investigate the connections between the variables in your data. Are you looking for correlations, group comparisons, or hierarchical structures to display? Your decision of visualization approaches will be influenced by an understanding of these linkages.

Specify your goals.

In order to select the best visualization style, it is crucial to clearly define your goals and the insights you wish to communicate. Think about the following inquiries:

What is the primary message or narrative you want to tell with your data?

What specific trends, comparisons, or patterns do you want to draw attention to?

What amount of specificity is required to properly communicate your message?

By responding to these inquiries, you will be better able to determine the goal of your vision and decide on the technique that will help you achieve it.

Take a look at the data attributes

Each visualization method has advantages and disadvantages when it comes to displaying particular data properties. When selecting your visualization method, take into account the following qualities:

Data Dimensionality:

Choose how many variables or dimensions you want to portray. Techniques like parallel coordinates or heatmaps may be appropriate if you have a lot of variables. Scatter plots or bar charts might be useful for data that has fewer dimensions.

Examine the level of depth or granularity you want to represent in your visualization. Techniques like aggregating data into histograms or using summary statistics may be appropriate if you have vast datasets. Individual data points can be visualized using methods like scatter plots or dot plots for more detailed data.

Data Scale:

Take your data's scale into account. Is it logarithmic, continuous, or discrete? For continuous data, visualization techniques like line charts or scatter plots are appropriate, but bar charts or treemaps are suited for discontinuous data.

Audience and Situation:

It's important to comprehend your target audience and the situation in which your visualization will be used. Think about the following elements:

Determine your audience's background information, including their level of data and visualization style familiarity. Select strategies that your target audience can use and will comprehend.

Medium and Context:

Select the platform on which you will present your visualization. Will it appear as a report, a presentation, or a dashboard that is interactive? To select the best visualization techniques, take into account the limitations of the medium and the available space.

Telling stories:

Consider the story or narrative you wish to illustrate with your image. Select strategies that highlight the most crucial features of the data and fit the narrative flow.

Iterate and try new things:

Don't be scared to try out various visualization methods and iterate. Sometimes a method that at first glance looks appropriate will not successfully convey your insights. Investigate alternative possibilities, develop prototypes, and get input from stakeholders or coworkers. You can produce the most powerful visualization of your data by iterating and improving your visualizations.

An essential first step in effectively presenting your data-driven insights is picking the appropriate visualization methods. You can choose the best visualization strategy by comprehending your data, setting your objectives, taking into account the data features, comprehending your audience, and trying out various ways. A strong tool for telling captivating data tales is visualization, so choose your choices carefully and let your data speak graphically.

Making Powerful Charts and Graphs: Impactful Data Visualization

Data can be presented in an engaging and informative manner using charts and graphs, which are effective tools. When utilized properly, they can improve comprehension, identify trends, and clearly express complex information. This chapter will examine important guidelines and best practices for producing graphs and charts that successfully communicate your data-driven message.

Recognize Your Message and Data

It is crucial to have a clear grasp of your data and the message you want to express before making a chart or graph. Think about the following:

Decide if your data are categorized or numerical in order to proceed. While numerical data consists of quantifiable amounts, categorical data reflects discrete categories. Each type of data is better represented by a different chart type.

Determine the connections between your data's variables. Do you wish to display contrasts, historical trends, or correlations? Your decision on the type of chart depends on your understanding of these relationships.

Identify the key takeaways or themes you wish to get across. This will enable you to focus your chart and make sure it conveys the message you want it to.

Select the Proper Chart Type. Effective data representation depends on choosing the right chart type. Think about the following typical chart types:

Bar Charts: For comparing categorical data or showing discrete values, bar charts are ideal. Use bars to indicate each category or value, either horizontal or vertical.

Line charts: Excellent for displaying temporal patterns and changes. To see the progression, draw lines connecting the data points.

Pie charts: These are helpful for showing percentages and proportions. To depict distinct categories and their varying sizes, divide a circle into sectors.

Scatter Plots: These are excellent for displaying the connection between two numerical variables. To find patterns or correlations, plot data points on a coordinate system.

Region Charts: These are similar to line charts but emphasize the magnitude of values over time by filling the region underneath the line.

Histograms: By classifying values into intervals and showing the frequency of occurrence, they illustrate the distribution of numerical data.

Heatmaps: A color-coded matrix is used to display data, making it easy to see patterns or connections in vast datasets.

Distinguish and Focus

Focus on the most crucial features of your data and simplify your design to produce excellent charts and graphs. Think about the following:

Data Labels and Axes: To help with context and understanding, clearly label your data points, categories, and axes.

Include meaningful titles and captions that communicate the goal and message of your chart in your chart.

Gridlines and Ticks: Use gridlines and ticks sparingly to direct the viewer's attention and make the chart easier to read.

Avoid Chart Junk: Remove extraneous components that don't aid in the comprehension of the data. Maintain a neat and clutter-free chart.

Utilize Visual Hierarchy And Color: When used effectively, color may improve charts and convey meaning. Think about the following:

Color Scheme: Pick a color scheme that complements the goal of your chart and is aesthetically pleasing. Make sure that colorblind viewers may readily discern and access the colors.

Highlighting: Use color to draw attention to certain statistics, patterns, or classifications. This can highlight important details and support the telling of an engaging story.

Visual Hierarchy: To build a hierarchy within your chart and direct the viewer's attention to the most crucial information, use color and other visual components.

Set The Scene And Offer An Interpretation: Your charts and graphs must be easily understood in their context, and interpretation is essential. Think about the following:

To offer context and prevent confusion, clearly name your axes and include units of measurement.

Use legends and annotations to describe any symbols, colors, or acronyms that are used in your chart.

Describe where you got your data from and what time frame it reflects. This increases validity and permits accurate interpretation.

Include captions and descriptions that highlight the key conclusions or insights from your graphic.

Understanding your data, choosing the appropriate chart types, simplifying the design, employing color efficiently, and offering context and interpretation are all skills that go into making great charts and graphs. You may produce visualizations that enthrall your audience, aid in understanding, and effectively communicate your data-driven insights by adhering to these principles and best practices.

Interactive and Dynamic Visualizations: Engaging and Exploring Data in Real-Time

Static charts and graphs are making way for dynamic, interactive visualizations that let users interact with data in real-time in the field of data visualization. Users can explore and examine data from various perspectives, find hidden patterns, and acquire deeper insights via interactive visualizations. We will explore the advantages, methods, and best practices of interactive and dynamic visualizations in this chapter in order to produce interesting data experiences.

The Power of Interactivity

Users can interact with data through interactive visualizations, making the experience more immersive and interesting. The following are a few major benefits of interactive visualizations:

Users can delve down into the data, filter particular dimensions, and dynamically alter parameters to see trends, outliers, and linkages that could go undetected in static displays.

With interactive visualizations, users may instantly apply filters to focus on particular subsets of data for more in-depth analysis. This adaptability facilitates iterative analysis and improves data exploration.

Users can access supplementary data, tooltips, or pop-ups that provide context and details about particular data points thanks to interactivity. Contextual knowledge improves comprehension and supports decision-making.

Interactive visualizations encourage active exploration and a sense of engagement by enabling users to manipulate and interact with data.

Approaches to Interactivity

To generate interactive and dynamic visualizations, a variety of features and techniques can be used. Think about the following:

Choose data points of interest, filter data based on particular criteria, and highlight particular categories. You can now concentrate on pertinent information and carry out focused analysis thanks to this.

Connect different visuals so that choosing data in one visualization shows related data in others. Users can investigate connections and correlations across various dimensions using this method.

Provide consumers with the option to pan through sizable datasets or zoom in and out of displays. This makes it possible to examine particular locations or interest areas in great detail.

When hovering over data points, these features show more information or context-specific details. Pop-ups and tooltips offer information without clogging the visualization.

Include interactive controls to allow users to dynamically change parameters and observe various facets of the data, such as sliders, drop-down menus, or checkboxes.

Guide to Interactive Visualization Best Practices

The following best practices should be taken into account while creating interactive visualizations:

Keep it Simple:

Make sure the interactive features are simple to understand and use. The visualization should be easy for users to navigate, filter, and interact with without creating a lot of unnecessary learning curves.

Offer Feedback:

When consumers interact with the data, provide them with visible feedback. The user experience is improved by highlighting particular data points, updating graphics in real-time, and offering dynamic tooltips.

Performance Optimization:

Enhance interactive visualizations' responsiveness, particularly when working with huge datasets. Think about methods like precomputation, data aggregation, or applying responsive design principles.

Mobile-Friendly Design:

Create interactive visualizations that are responsive and simple to use across a range of screen sizes, given the rising use of mobile devices.

Test and Iterate:

Test your interactive visualizations with your intended audience to receive feedback and spot any flaws. Iterate to improve usability and efficiency depending on user feedback.

Data is brought to life through interactive and dynamic visualizations, enabling users to explore and discover new information in real-time. You can design interesting data experiences that encourage exploration, comprehension, and decision-making by including interactive elements, utilizing strategies like filtering, brushing and connecting, zooming, and offering contextual information.

Chapter Eight: Machine Learning

The Future of Data-Driven Intelligence: Unleashing the Power of Machine Learning

Welcome to the fascinating field of machine learning, where computer programs learn from data to anticipate future events, spot patterns, and find undiscovered information. Machine learning has become a revolutionary force in today's data-driven world, transforming entire industries and paving the way for ground-breaking advances in artificial intelligence. In this chapter, we will explore the principles of machine learning, including its fundamental ideas, practical uses, and amazing future-shaping potential.

Consider a situation where you have a ton of data but are unable to meaningfully analyze it or forecast the future with any degree of accuracy. Let's talk about machine learning, a discipline that gives computers the capacity to automatically learn from data and enhance their performance without explicit programming. Giving robots the capacity to spot complex patterns, forecast results, and make defensible decisions based on the available facts is like to giving them superpowers.

Algorithms, which are complex mathematical models created to identify patterns, correlations, and trends in data, are at the core of machine learning. These algorithms are remarkably effective and scalable while simulating the human learning process. Machine learning algorithms can uncover hidden insights, identify subtle patterns, and produce accurate forecasts by analyzing enormous amounts of data. This allows businesses, researchers, and individuals to confidently make decisions based on data.

There are numerous domains in which machine learning is used. It can help with disease diagnosis, patient outcome prediction, and developing individualized treatment regimens in the field of healthcare. It drives credit risk evaluation tools, algorithmic trading models, and fraud detection systems in finance. In marketing, it enables companies to give individualized advice, optimize marketing initiatives, and comprehend consumer behavior. Machine learning is transforming our environment and opening the door for unimaginable technological developments, from self-driving cars to virtual assistants.

Let's explore the two main divisions of machine learning—supervised learning and unsupervised learning—in order to understand its essence.

In supervised learning, input data and corresponding output labels are linked up to train a model on labeled data. The objective is for the model to understand the relationship between inputs and outputs so that it can accurately predict outcomes from brand-new, untainted data. It's like having a teacher who will guide your learning and give you feedback on how accurate your predictions were.

The model in unsupervised learning, on the other hand, searches for innate patterns, structures, or groupings in the unlabeled data. Without explicit instructions, the model scours the data landscape in search of significant connections and clusters. Giving the model a blank canvas and letting it create its own interpretation of the data is the analogy for unsupervised learning.

We have access to a wide range of machine learning algorithms within these areas. Every technique, from decision trees to support vector machines to neural networks to deep learning architectures, has its advantages and is best suited for a certain class of problems. The type of data, the intended result, and the resources accessible all influence the algorithm that is chosen.

The journey of machine learning entails data investigation, model construction, and ongoing improvement. Data preparation, feature engineering, model choice, training, evaluation, and fine-tuning are all part of the process. It calls for a fusion of programming abilities, statistical knowledge, domain understanding, and a good helping of creativity and curiosity.

Prepare to see the amazing skills of algorithms as we set off on this journey through the realm of machine learning. These algorithms have the ability to see patterns that are invisible to the human eye, forecast the future with astonishing accuracy, and unearth insights hidden deep within mountains of data. To create a better future, let's jointly realize the potential of machine learning and harness the strength of data-driven intelligence.

Supervised and Unsupervised Learning: Unleashing the Power of Data-driven Discovery

Two main strategies—supervised learning and unsupervised learning—dominate the field of machine learning. Each of these methods, with its special qualities and uses, offers strong instruments for drawing insights and patterns from data. Let's explore the concepts, applications, and examples of supervised and unsupervised learning to better understand their capabilities.

Supervised Learning: Using Labeled Data

Training a model on labeled data, where each data point is accompanied by a corresponding output label or goal variable, is the basis of supervised learning. The objective is for the model to learn the relationship between the inputs and the corresponding outputs so that it can make precise predictions about brand-new, untainted data.

Let's look at a well-known example of supervised learning—classifying email spam—to better grasp it. Consider a collection of many emails where each email is classified as either "spam" or "not spam." The input data consists of a variety of elements, including the email's sender, subject, and body. This tagged data is used to train a supervised learning algorithm, which then trains the model to distinguish between spam and non-spam emails. After being trained, the model may categorize fresh incoming emails as spam or not depending on the patterns it has discovered.

The prediction of home values is another use of supervised learning. A supervised learning algorithm can be trained to forecast the price of a new house based on its features given a dataset of houses with variables like the number of bedrooms, square footage, and location, as well as their related sale prices. This makes it possible for purchasers or real estate brokers to determine the worth of a property before completing a purchase.

The availability of labeled data, which acts as the model's "teacher" in supervised learning, is a key component. The model may generalize and make predictions on fresh, new samples by learning from this labeled data. Decision trees, logistic regression, support vector machines (SVM), and linear regression are examples of supervised learning techniques.

Supervised Learning: Discerning the Unknown

Unsupervised learning, as contrast to supervised learning, works with unlabeled data, and the model attempts to identify underlying patterns, structures, or clusters without any explicit direction. Unsupervised learning algorithms work on the premise that knowledge can be gained from the data's innate structure.

Let's look at a customer segmentation task as an example of unsupervised learning. Consider that you have a collection of customer transaction records that include data on demographics, browsing habits, and past purchases. The program can find groups of comparable customers based on their purchase behaviors and preferences by utilizing an unsupervised learning approach, such as k-means clustering or hierarchical clustering. Businesses can target particular consumer segments with tailored marketing tactics thanks to this segmentation.

Anomaly detection is another illustration of unsupervised learning. Imagine you wish to find fraudulent activity in a dataset of credit card transactions. An unsupervised learning system that has been trained can identify the typical patterns of legitimate transactions and flag any strange or anomalous ones as possible cases of fraud.

Even in cases when the underlying labels or categories are unknown, unsupervised learning algorithms concentrate on sifting out significant patterns and structures from the data. They include of Gaussian mixture models (GMM), principal component analysis (PCA), and clustering algorithms for dimensionality reduction.

The Effectiveness of Combined Methods

You should be aware that supervised and unsupervised learning are not mutually exclusive; you can combine the two to get more information from the data. Unsupervised learning approaches, for instance, can be used to explore and preprocess the data in order to find hidden structures or to reduce its dimensionality. A supervised learning algorithm can then be trained to produce precise predictions or classifications using the altered data.

A smaller amount of labeled data is accessible alongside a larger collection of unlabeled data in semi-supervised learning procedures, as well. As a result, the model can take use of the sparse labeled data to enhance performance while also gaining access to the enormous unlabeled data set for exploration and pattern recognition.

In conclusion, while unsupervised learning uses unlabeled data to discover underlying patterns and structures, supervised learning thrives on labeled data, enabling precise prediction and classification tasks. Combining the two ways can provide even more potent insights and discoveries from data, as each has unique benefits and uses.

Let's embrace the promise of both supervised and unsupervised learning as we continue our exploration of the world of machine learning, pushing the bounds of what is conceivable and utilizing the strength of data-driven discovery.

Evaluating the Stars of Machine Learning: Unveiling the Metrics for Model Mastery

Constructing a model is simply the beginning of the adventure in the fascinating realm of machine learning. The real test comes from assessing how well it performs and achieves its intended goals. Evaluation metrics are useful instruments that enable us to judge the potency and dependability of our machine learning models in this context. In this chapter, we set out on an enlightening tour of assessment metrics, learning about their complexities, practical uses, and the tips and tricks they may provide for mastering models.

We require a yardstick to gauge the success of machine learning models while assessing them. Accuracy, which calculates the proportion of accurately predicted instances among all instances, is one of the most popular evaluation metrics. While accuracy offers a broad picture of the model's performance, it may not be enough in cases where the data are unbalanced or mistakes of different kinds have distinct effects.

Precision and memory help to overcome these restrictions. Out of all positive predictions, precision is the percentage of true positives (positive cases that were correctly identified). When the model asserts that something is positive, it informs us of how well the model performs. The fraction of true positives out of all real positive cases is measured by recall, on the other hand. It reveals how effectively the model captures all instances of positivity in the data. When dealing with circumstances where false positives or false negatives may have important repercussions, these measures are especially helpful.

Let's use an illustration to illustrate these measurements. Consider developing a model to identify unauthorized credit card transactions. Precision is essential in this situation. We want to reduce false positives since erroneously labeling legal transactions as fraudulent can cause customers to experience unneeded inconveniences. However, recall is also crucial since we want to stop as many fraudulent transactions as we can to safeguard both customers and the company. In these situations, finding the ideal balance between memory and precision is crucial.

But what if we also need to consider recall while weighing precision? The F1 score is relevant in this situation. The F1 score, which combines precision and recall into a single metric, is the harmonic mean of these two metrics. It is helpful in situations where we want to identify the best trade-off between recall and precision.

Other evaluation metrics adapted to certain machine learning tasks are available in addition to accuracy, precision, recall, and F1 score. For instance, mean absolute error (MAE) and root mean square error (RMSE) are frequently utilized in regression situations. While RMSE takes the square root of the average squared difference, MAE measures the average absolute difference between the predicted and actual values. These measures help us determine the size of mistakes by revealing how well the model's predictions match the actual values.

Additionally, metrics like the area under the ROC curve (AUC-ROC) and precision-recall curve are useful in classification issues with imbalanced data, when one class predominates the dataset. The precision-recall curve illustrates the trade-off between precision and recall at various classification levels, while AUC-ROC gauges the model's ability to discriminate between positive and negative instances across various thresholds. These measurements are especially helpful in situations when class imbalance makes it difficult to evaluate models accurately.

It's important to remember that evaluation measures are task-specific and based on the specifics of the current issue. Different assessment metrics provide information on many facets of model performance, whether it be in sentiment analysis, picture recognition, fraud detection, or disease diagnosis.

Our objective as machine learning practitioners is to select the evaluation metrics that are best suited to solving the particular issue at hand and to interpret the outcomes accordingly. The metrics chosen should be in line with the task's goals, the significance of various fault types, and the underlying context.

When evaluating machine learning models, various evaluation metrics can be employed depending on the specific task and problem domain. Here is a list of commonly used evaluation metrics for different types of machine learning models:

Classification Metrics

Accuracy: Measures the proportion of correctly classified instances.

Precision: Calculates the proportion of true positives out of all positive predictions.

Recall: Measures the proportion of true positives out of all actual positive instances.

F1 Score: Harmonic mean of precision and recall, providing a balanced measure.

Area Under the ROC Curve (AUC-ROC): Evaluates the model's ability to discriminate between positive and negative instances across different thresholds.

Precision-Recall Curve: Illustrates the trade-off between precision and recall at different classification thresholds.

Log Loss: Measures the logarithmic loss between predicted probabilities and true class labels.

Regression Metrics:

Mean Absolute Error (MAE): Computes the average absolute difference between predicted and actual values.

Root Mean Square Error (RMSE): Calculates the square root of the average squared difference between predicted and actual values.

Mean Squared Error (MSE): Computes the average of the squared difference between predicted and actual values.

R-squared (R^2): Measures the proportion of the variance in the dependent variable explained by the model.

Clustering Metrics:

Silhouette Coefficient: Quantifies the compactness and separation of clusters.

Calinski-Harabasz Index: Evaluates the ratio of between-cluster dispersion to within-cluster dispersion.

Davies-Bouldin Index: Measures the average similarity between clusters and their nearest neighboring cluster.

Ranking Metrics:

Mean Average Precision (MAP): Calculates the average precision across different recall levels.

Normalized Discounted Cumulative Gain (NDCG): Assesses the quality of ranked recommendations.

Precision at K: Measures the proportion of relevant items in the top K recommendations.

Anomaly Detection Metrics:

True Positive Rate (TPR): Measures the proportion of true anomalies correctly identified.

False Positive Rate (FPR): Calculates the proportion of false positives identified as anomalies.

Area Under the ROC Curve (AUC-ROC): Evaluates the model's performance in distinguishing anomalies from normal instances.

It's important to note that these metrics are not exhaustive, and there may be domain-specific metrics or variations of the above metrics depending on the problem at hand. Choosing the appropriate evaluation metrics requires understanding the specific goals, constraints, and nuances of the machine learning task.

Remember that evaluation metrics provide valuable insights into model performance and guide the selection and optimization of models to achieve desired outcomes.

Chapter Nine: Big Data Analytics

Navigating the Depths of Information: Unveiling the Power of Big Data

The quantity, speed, and variety of data being produced in today's connected world are increasing to previously unthinkable proportions. This avalanche of data, dubbed "big data," offers both amazing benefits and overwhelming challenges. Let's explore big data's definition, problems, and transformational effects on businesses and society as we set off on this thrilling voyage through this world.

Big data mostly refers to enormous and complex datasets that can't be processed and analyzed using conventional data processing and analysis techniques. It includes a wide range of data kinds, including structured, unstructured, and semi-structured data as well as streaming data from sensors and gadgets, posts from social media, multimedia, and much more. Big data has volumes measured in terabytes, petabytes, and even exabytes, making its sheer size mind-boggling.

Let's look at an example to better grasp the importance of big data. Consider a massive retailer that serves millions of clients online. It gathers information on client transactions, internet interactions, social media interactions, and supply chain activities every day. This vast amount of data has a wealth of insights that, if correctly tapped into, can result in better customer experiences, focused marketing efforts, improved inventory management, and improved business decision-making.

The process of gaining value from big data is difficult, though. Managing the rate at which data is generated is one of the main issues. Data streams in real time from a variety of sources in the digital age, including social media sites, Internet of Things (IoT) gadgets, and online transactions. Organizations must use scalable and effective data processing methods to handle the constant influx of information due to the speed at which this data is produced.

The handling of the variety of data presents another difficulty. Big data includes both structured and unstructured data, including text documents, photos, videos, and social media posts. Structured data examples include customer information and transactional data. It need sophisticated tools and processes that can handle the complexity and diversity of information to integrate and analyze these dissimilar data sources.

Big data also poses problems with regard to data quality or truthfulness. Due to the enormous volume of data being produced, it is essential to make sure the data is accurate, full, and reliable. Incomplete or inaccurate data can result in incorrect insights and poor decision-making. To address these issues and guarantee data integrity, it is crucial to implement data cleansing, validation, and quality assurance processes.

Big data also prompts worries about data security and privacy. The protection of people's privacy and the confidentiality of sensitive information is crucial when businesses gather and analyze enormous volumes of personal data. To preserve trust and confidence in the digital era, firms must continue to face issues including protecting data from cyber threats and adhering to regulatory obligations.

Big data has enormous potential advantages despite these difficulties. It has the potential to change a number of industries, including manufacturing, healthcare, banking, and transportation. For instance, big data analytics in healthcare can find patterns and connections in clinical trial data and medical records, enabling better illness diagnosis, individualized treatment, and preventative healthcare measures.

By evaluating massive amounts of transactional data in real-time, big data analytics allows for the detection of fraudulent actions in the financial sector. Additionally, it makes risk modeling and prediction easier, enabling financial organizations to plan ahead and run their businesses more efficiently.

Big data is also crucial in "smart cities," which use information from sensors, traffic cameras, and social media platforms to optimize transit routes, boost energy efficiency, and improve public safety.

Big data has a lot of potential, but navigating its depths necessitates addressing difficulties with regard to speed, diversity, veracity, and security. Organizations can realize the revolutionary power of big data by adopting cutting-edge technologies like distributed computing, cloud computing, and machine learning. Let's use the power of big data as we set out on this exciting journey to gather insightful knowledge, spur innovation, and create a brighter future for businesses and society as a whole.

Technologies for Processing and Analyzing Big Data

In the fascinating world of big data, where large volumes of information are generated at a pace that has never been seen before, the technologies that are used to handle and analyze this data play an essential part in the extraction of useful insights. Let's get started on a tour of some of the most prominent technologies that give businesses the ability to overcome the problems of processing and analyzing large data.

Apache Hadoop:

Apache Hadoop is a foundational technology in the big data landscape. The Hadoop Distributed File System (HDFS) and the MapReduce processing framework are the two primary components that make up this system. HDFS makes it possible to store big datasets in a distributed manner across clusters of commodity hardware, while MapReduce makes it possible to process data in parallel so that computations may be performed on the data. Processing and analyzing enormous amounts of data is one of Hadoop's strengths because to the platform's fault-tolerant architecture and scalability. It has developed into

119

the central pillar of many big data initiatives, providing businesses with the ability to store, process, and derive insights from enormous datasets.

Apache Spark:

Apache Spark is a framework for processing large amounts of data that is both powerful and flexible. Because it is capable of high-speed processing in memory as well as processing enormous amounts of data, it is ideally suited for handling large-scale data analytics workloads. Spark offers a single analytics engine that is capable of supporting a variety of data processing paradigms. These processing paradigms include batch processing, real-time streaming, machine learning, and graph processing. Its extensive ecosystem of libraries, which includes Spark SQL, MLlib, and GraphX, further increases its capabilities and makes it possible for enterprises to do in-depth data analysis in a time-efficient manner.

Apache Kafka:

Apache Kafka is a distributed streaming platform that excels at handling high-throughput, fault-tolerant, and real-time data streaming. It enables businesses to collect, store, and interpret enormous amounts of data coming from a variety of sources, including sensors, social media feeds, and transactional systems, amongst others. Because Kafka's publish-subscribe format enables numerous applications to consume data streams in simultaneously, it has become a popular choice for the construction of real-time data pipelines and applications that do streaming analytics.

Cloud Computing Platforms:

Cloud computing platforms, such as Amazon Web Services (AWS), Microsoft Azure, and Google Cloud Platform (GCP), provide scalable infrastructure and services tailored for big data processing and analysis. These platforms offer managed services, such as Amazon EMR, Azure HDInsight, and Google Cloud Dataproc, which simplify the deployment and management of big data frameworks like Hadoop and Spark. Examples of these managed services are Amazon EMR, Azure HDInsight, and Google Cloud Dataproc. Taking use of the cloud's elasticity and scalability, enterprises are able to dynamically supply resources to manage shifting workloads and extend their data processing capabilities as required. This allows them to better meet customer demands.

NoSQL Databases:

In the area of big data, NoSQL databases have become increasingly popular as a result of their capacity to manage huge amounts of data while maintaining low latency and high availability. MongoDB and Apache Cassandra are two examples of such databases. Because these databases offer flexible data models and horizontal scalability, they are suited for use cases that involve the storing, retrieval, and real-time analysis of enormous amounts of data. They provide a high throughput for both reading and writing, making it possible for businesses to efficiently manage data-intensive operations.

Technologies for Data Warehousing:

Data warehousing technologies, such as Apache Hive and Amazon Redshift, give businesses the ability to efficiently store and analyze both structured and semi-structured data. In order to achieve great performance when querying enormous datasets, these technologies make use of columnar storage, various strategies for compression, and query optimization. They give an interface that is similar to SQL, which makes it simpler for analysts and data scientists to work with big data using tools and languages they are already familiar with.

Frameworks for Machine Learning:

In the process of gleaning insights from large amounts of data, machine learning plays an important role. Building and training machine learning models on huge datasets is made easier with the use of strong tools made available by frameworks like as TensorFlow, PyTorch, and scikit-learn. These frameworks handle big data analytics by utilizing techniques from distributed computing. As a result, businesses are able to discover patterns in their data, formulate predictions based on those patterns, and obtain deeper insights from their data.

Data Visualization Tools:

Data visualization tools, such as Tableau, Power BI, and D3.js, make it easier to display and explore the insights that may be gleaned from large amounts of data in a way that is visually attractive. These tools enable analysts and stakeholders to interact with data through the use of user-friendly dashboards, charts, and graphs, which in turn enables them to draw significant insights in a short amount of time. Through the process of data visualization, firms are able to effectively express the intricate patterns and trends that are buried inside their huge databases.

Each of these technologies contributes significantly to the handling and examination of massive amounts of data. Organizations are able to manage the complexity of big data, discover patterns that were previously hidden, and make decisions that are driven by data in order to achieve both corporate growth and innovation when they leverage their skills.

Building the Foundation for Big Data Success: Unlocking the Power of Scalable Data Storage and Retrieval

Scalable data storage and retrieval solutions are essential in the world of big data, where enormous amounts of information are produced and consumed at an unprecedented rate. Organizations must implement scalable strategies that can meet the expanding demands of big data because traditional data storage technologies are unable to handle the sheer amount and velocity of data. The topic of scalable data storage and retrieval is explored in this chapter, along with a number of technologies and methods that enable businesses to effectively manage, store, and access large datasets.

Distributed File Systems:

Scalable data storage is based on distributed file systems. These systems split data among numerous computers, enabling parallel processing and effective storage. The Hadoop Distributed File System (HDFS) is a well-known example. By dividing enormous datasets into blocks and distributing them across a cluster of commodity hardware, HDFS is made to handle large datasets. In order to provide fault tolerance and high availability, HDFS stores data redundantly across several nodes.

NoSOL Databases:

NoSQL databases have become a popular option for scalable data storage and retrieval. NoSQL (Not Only SQL) databases. NoSQL databases provide horizontal scalability and flexible schemas in contrast to conventional relational databases. Massive amounts of structured, semi-structured, and unstructured data can be handled by them. MongoDB, Apache HBase, and Apache Cassandra are a few examples. To achieve great scalability and performance, these databases use distributed architectures, data partitioning, and replication.

Key-Value Stores:

Another category of scalable data storage options is the key-value store. They offer a straightforward yet effective model for data retrieval and storage. Key-value databases, like Apache Redis and Amazon DynamoDB, provide quick retrieval based on keys and store data as key-value pairs. Because of their high throughput and low latency, these stores are well suited for use cases including caching, session management, and real-time analytics where quick data access is essential.

Columnar databases:

These databases are made to store and retrieve data as efficiently and quickly as possible for analytical workloads. Column-wise data storage enables effective compression and enhances query performance. Google Bigtable and Apache Cassandra are two examples. Columnar databases are ideal for data warehousing, business intelligence, and data analytics applications since they execute aggregations and massive dataset management exceptionally well.

Object Storage:

Object storage is a scalable and economical method for storing enormous amounts of unstructured data. It offers a flat address space for accessing and managing data and organizes the data as objects. Systems for object storage, like Amazon S3 and Google Cloud Storage, provide practically infinite scalability and durability. They are frequently used to store backups, log data, multimedia material, and files. Big data architectures can be built on a solid, highly scalable basis provided by object storage.

Distributed in-memory storage:

To enable quick data access, distributed in-memory storage systems make use of RAM on a number of computers. Hazelcast and Apache Ignite are two examples. These systems save data in-memory, making it possible to analyze and query data instantly. They are ideal for applications like real-time analytics, caching, and high-performance computing that call for low-latency access to frequently accessed data.

Data indexing and search:

Technologies for indexing and searching data are essential for effectively obtaining data from big datasets.

Data may be quickly and precisely retrieved using search engines like Elasticsearch and Apache Solr. They use relevance ranking algorithms, distributed infrastructures, and indexing techniques to produce quick search results even for terabytes of data. Building search-driven applications, logging systems, and data exploration tools all depend on these technologies.

Organizations may get over the difficulties of handling and gaining access to huge data by implementing these scalable data storage and retrieval solutions. These technologies lay the groundwork for creating dependable and effective data structures that can manage the rapidly increasing volume and velocity of data produced in the modern digital era.

Chapter Ten: Data Analytics Ethical Considerations

Protecting Privacy, Bias, and Transparency in the Digital Age

Ethics play a critical role in assuring responsible and reliable use of information in the era of data analytics, when firms gather, analyze, and extract insights from large amounts of data. It is crucial to address the ethical issues that develop in the field of data analytics as data-driven technologies become more sophisticated and prevalent. In order to protect privacy, eliminate bias, and sustain transparency in data analytics, practitioners, researchers, and organizations must manage certain ethical issues, which are explored in this chapter.

Privacy protection:

In data analytics, privacy is a basic ethical concern. People have the right to control how their personal information is gathered, utilized, and disseminated. Subtopics include: a. Informed Consent: Prior to collecting and utilizing personal data, organizations must get informed consent from individuals. This entails outlining the data being gathered, the goals for which it will be used, and any possible hazards involved in plain and transparent terms.

Anonymization and De-identification:

To safeguard people's privacy, appropriate methods for anonymizing and de-identifying data must be used. To ensure that data cannot be connected back to specific individuals, this involves eliminating personally identifying information (PII) or using techniques like data masking or aggregation.

Data Security:

Data must be protected from illegal access, security breaches, and cyberthreats, so organizations must put in place strong security measures. To lessen the potential harm to people in the event of a data breach, quick notice and appropriate action must be performed.

Biases:

Data analytics bias can have serious societal repercussions and support unjust or discriminatory practices, hence it must be minimized. Biases that result from data collection, preprocessing, and modeling must be addressed.

Bias in Data Collection: Biases can occur throughout the data collection process, resulting in skewed or unrepresentative datasets. To prevent reinforcing preexisting prejudices, organizations should strive for diversity and inclusivity in data collecting.

Algorithmic Bias: When used with data that already contains biases, machine learning algorithms may unintentionally magnify those biases. It is crucial to routinely check algorithms for bias and implement corrective measures to lessen discrimination.

Justice and Equity:

Organizations should work to ensure justice and equity in data-driven decision-making processes. This entails identifying and resolving any potential disparate effects on various groups as well as making sure that decisions don't lead to unfair benefits or disadvantages.

Transparency:

Building trust and responsibility in data analytics requires transparency and explainability, both of which are essential.

Model Transparency: Organizations should work to make their data analytics models clear and understandable so that they may shed light on the decision-making process. This enables people to comprehend and consider the driving forces behind outcomes.

Interpretability: Complex machine learning models must be made understandable so that stakeholders can comprehend the elements and variables that went into making predictions or taking choices. This encourages responsibility and faith in the judgment process.

Auditing and Accountability: To guarantee adherence to moral standards, routine audits of data analytics methods, models, and algorithms should be carried out. Organizations should take responsibility for the results of their data analytics projects and be prepared to address any problems or biases that are found.

Data Governance and Regulation:

Strong data governance frameworks and regulatory procedures can help to further protect the integrity of data analytics operations. The following are some of the subtopics: a. Data Governance: Organizations should set up clear policies, methods, and guidelines for managing data, including data collection, storage, use, and sharing. Frameworks for data governance make ensuring that data is handled ethically and responsibly throughout its existence.

Legal and Regulatory Compliance: Organizations are required to abide by all applicable laws and rules pertaining to the privacy, security, and protection of data. Examples include the California Consumer Privacy Act (CCPA) in the United States and the General Data Protection Regulation (GDPR) in Europe. These rules' observance guarantees that data analytics operations are compliant with the law and safeguard persons' rights.

Creating internal or external ethical review boards can assist firms in assessing and addressing the ethical implications of their data analytics projects. c. These boards offer monitoring, direction, and recommendations to make sure moral standards are upheld.

For the sake of preserving trust, safeguarding privacy, averting bias, and fostering transparency, ethical considerations in data analytics are essential. To ensure responsible and accountable use of data, organizations must traverse these considerations. Organizations can create moral data analytics frameworks that help people and society at large by putting a priority on privacy protection, reducing biases, fostering transparency, and adhering to the rules that apply.

Chapter Eleven: Data Analytics in Business

Unleashing the Power of Data for Informed Decision-making

Welcome to the world of business data analytics! Today's digital era has flooded organizations with enormous amounts of data. For businesses in a variety of industries, the ability to derive actionable insights from this data has changed the game. This chapter will examine the use of data analytics across various industries, the significance of key business metrics in analytics-driven decision making, and data-driven storytelling as a tool for effective communication.

Applications of Data Analytics in Various Industries

Retail and e-commerce:

Data analytics has completely changed these sectors of the economy, allowing businesses to optimize their processes and improve customer experiences. For instance, online retailers look at customer demographics, purchase history, and browsing habits to provide specialized product recommendations and focused advertising. They use data to pinpoint market trends, enhance pricing approaches, and effectively manage inventory.

Healthcare:

Data analytics is essential for improving patient outcomes and allocating resources efficiently. Hospitals can use patient information, medical records, and clinical research, for instance, to create predictive models for disease diagnosis and treatment improvement. Patient vitals monitored in real-time can help identify anomalies and offer prompt interventions. Healthcare professionals can analyze population health trends, spot disease outbreaks, and allocate resources more efficiently with the aid of data analytics.

Finance and Banking:

To guide strategic decision-making, manage risks, and provide individualized financial services, the finance and banking sector heavily relies on data analytics. For instance, by examining patterns and anomalies, credit card companies use data analytics to find fraudulent transactions. Banks employ customer data to construct credit scoring models, determine loan eligibility, and make data-driven investment decisions. Furthermore, data analytics helps financial institutions comply with regulatory standards and analyze market developments.

Manufacturing and Supply Chain:

Data analytics has altered the manufacturing and supply chain business by enhancing operating efficiency, cutting costs, and maintaining quality control. Manufacturers evaluate production data to detect bottlenecks, enhance operations, and minimize downtime. They employ predictive maintenance models to anticipate equipment faults in advance, saving maintenance costs and enhancing overall productivity. Supply chain management benefits from data analytics by optimizing inventory levels, enhancing logistics planning, and reducing delivery times.

Marketing and Advertising:

Data analytics has transformed marketing and advertising techniques, enabling firms to provide customized adverts and optimize their return on investment. Marketers evaluate customer data, social media trends, and online behavior to find target audiences and adapt advertising messaging. They employ data analytics to analyze the efficiency of marketing initiatives, track key performance indicators, and make real-time modifications to maximize their marketing budget.

Key Business Metrics and Analytics-driven Decision-making

Revenue and Profitability:

Revenue and profitability measurements are at the basis of corporate success. Data analytics helps firms to examine revenue sources, pricing tactics, and client segmentation to drive revenue growth. For example, an e-commerce company can examine sales data to find high-margin products, refine pricing models, and conduct targeted cross-selling or upselling initiatives. By analyzing client purchase trends and preferences, firms can maximize their revenue.

Customer Acquisition and Retention:

Customer acquisition and retention are crucial for sustainable business success. Organizations can use data analytics to determine the most important customer categories and create strategies for acquiring and keeping customers. Organizations may personalize marketing messaging, develop specialized offers, and improve the entire consumer experience by evaluating customer data. A telecom corporation, for instance, can use customer behavior analysis to forecast attrition, enabling proactive retention strategies like tailored offers or proactive customer care.

Operational Efficiency:

In the current fast-paced corporate world, operational efficiency is essential for firms to stay competitive. Organizations may find inefficiencies, allocate resources more efficiently, and improve operations thanks to data analytics. For instance, a manufacturing business can utilize data analytics to track the operation of its equipment, identify maintenance requirements, and schedule proactive maintenance tasks. As a result, costs are kept to a minimum and production efficiency is increased.

Risk Management:

Identifying, evaluating, and reducing risks are important aspects of running a business. Data analytics is a key tool in this process. Organizations can create predictive models that aid in the identification of possible hazards and the adoption of preventative actions to successfully manage them by studying historical data and market patterns. Insurance companies, for instance, utilize data analytics to evaluate risk profiles, establish premiums, and spot bogus claims.

Effective Communication and Data-driven Storytelling

For organizations to successfully communicate findings and spur action, data-driven storytelling is crucial. Key factors for good communication include the following:

Relevance and Context:

It is critical to take into account the audience while delivering data insights and to provide context that is consistent with their objectives. Organizations may direct decision-making and make sure that data-driven recommendations are actionable by concentrating on the most pertinent insights.

Visualization & Presentation:

Graphs, charts, and visualizations are effective tools for presenting data in an understandable and interesting way. Using the right visualization tools makes it easier to emphasize and make sense of important discoveries. For instance, a line graph can show trends over time while a bar chart can compare sales performance across several locations.

Creating Stories around Data Insights:

Using storytelling techniques, you can draw in the audience and make the relevance of the findings clear by creating a story around the data insights. Data-driven tales are made more approachable and powerful by linking the data insights to the organization's goals and problems. The narrative experience can be improved by employing tactics like using real-world examples, stories, and appealing images.

Actionable suggestions:

Data analytics should produce actionable suggestions in addition to insights. Clarifying the consequences of the insights and outlining specific actions that may be taken to seize opportunities or tackle obstacles are both important components of effective communication. Organizations are able to convert data insights into observable outcomes by offering actionable advice.

With the use of data analytics, businesses are now able to harness the power of data to make wise decisions. Data analytics is used in a wide range of sectors, from retail and healthcare to finance and marketing, transforming operations and spurring corporate expansion. Organizations can make data-driven decisions and improve performance by utilizing essential business KPIs. For the purpose of communicating findings, involving stakeholders, and motivating action, data-driven storytelling and communication are crucial. Businesses may open up new opportunities and establish a competitive edge in the data-driven era with the proper blend of data analytics, metrics-driven decision-making, and compelling storytelling.

Chapter Twelve: Tools and Platforms for Data Analytics

Facilitating Insights and Action

Welcome to the fascinating world of tools and resources for data analytics! In the modern era of data-driven decision-making, organizations have access to a wide range of tools and resources that allow them to gain insightful knowledge from their data. We will examine the landscape of data analytics tools and resources in this chapter, emphasizing their value, functionalities, and industrial applications.

Tools for data analytics are essential for converting raw data into insights that can be put to use. They give businesses the tools they need to handle, examine, and visualize data in an organized and effective way. By enabling users to find patterns, trends, and links within their data, these tools enable users to take wise decisions and promote corporate success. Organizations may use the power of data to acquire a competitive edge in their particular industries with the correct tools.

Important Functions of Data Analytics Tools

Data Cleansing and Integration:

Users of data analytics tools can combine data from a variety of sources, including databases, spreadsheets, and internet platforms. They offer tools for cleaning and transforming data, eliminating errors and inconsistencies. By ensuring that the analysis is founded on accurate and trustworthy data, data purification helps to produce more precise insights.

Data Visualization and Exploration:

One of the main advantages of data analytics technologies is their capacity for visual data exploration. Charts, graphs, and interactive dashboards are just a few of the many visualization possibilities that are available with these technologies. Users may easily spot trends, outliers, and correlations in the data with the aid of visual representations. Data visualization makes difficult ideas easier to understand and more useful.

Statistical Analysis and Modeling:

A variety of statistical analysis and modeling capabilities are offered by data analytics technologies.

Users can run a number of statistical tests, including clustering, regression analysis, and hypothesis testing. With the use of these tools, users may create predictive models that can detect key variables, forecast future trends, and make predictions based on data.

Machine learning and artificial intelligence:

A lot of cutting-edge data analytics tools use these two types of algorithms. These algorithms are able to forecast outcomes, classify data, and find patterns automatically. Organizations may derive deeper insights from their data and automate challenging analytical activities thanks to machine learning algorithms that evolve and improve over time.

Applications in Different Sectors

Tools for data analytics are used in a variety of industries, enabling businesses to learn more and spur innovation. Here are a few illustrations:

Retail and e-commerce:

To monitor consumer behavior, improve pricing strategies, and personalize marketing campaigns, retailers and e-commerce businesses utilize data analytics solutions.

These techniques aid with trend identification, consumer segmentation, and demand forecasting, all of which contribute to higher sales and happier customers.

Healthcare:

Analyzing patient data, enhancing clinical results, and allocating resources efficiently all need the use of data analytics tools. They aid in the identification of prospective health concerns, forecasting patient readmission rates, and illness diagnosis.

Finance and banking:

To analyze client data, spot fraud, and determine creditworthiness, financial firms use data analytics techniques. These instruments support regulatory compliance, risk assessment, and portfolio management.

Manufacturing and supply chain:

Data analytics tools help firms to streamline operations, cut costs, and guarantee quality. These solutions help supply chain management by streamlining operations, increasing logistics, and optimizing inventory levels.

Organizations' capacity to harness the power of data and make wise decisions is driven by data analytics tools and resources. They give firms the tools to integrate, analyze, display, and model data, enabling them to find insightful information and achieve a competitive edge. These tools offer a wide range of features to meet the needs of different businesses, from data exploration and visualization to statistical analysis and machine learning. Organizations may maximize the value of their data and pave the way for data-driven success by embracing data analytics technologies.

Predictive Analytics Tools

Welcome to the exciting world of predictive analytics tools! Businesses and organizations are increasingly depending on predictive analytics in today's data-driven world in order to gather insightful information, make wise choices, and remain ahead of the competition. Tools for predictive analytics give you the skills you need to find hidden patterns, predict outcomes, and implement data-driven strategies. We will examine the foundations of predictive analytics tools, their uses, and the essential characteristics that make them potent tools in the data analytics space in this chapter.

Tools for predictive analytics are made expressly to evaluate previous data, spot trends, and produce forecasts or projections for upcoming occurrences or results. These tools use cutting-edge statistical algorithms, machine learning methods, and data mining approaches to glean insightful information from massive volumes of data. Businesses can take preventive actions, reduce risks, and grasp opportunities by comprehending the links and trends concealed within the data.

Use cases for predictive analytics tools

Forecasting:

Forecasting is one of the main uses for predictive analytics tools. These technologies assist companies in accurately forecasting future events, ether it be customer behavior, sales patterns, market demand, or even prospective threats. Retailers, for example, might use predictive analytics to forecast customer demand for certain products, allowing them to manage inventory levels and schedule production appropriately. Financial institutions can utilize these technologies in a similar way to forecast creditworthiness and control risk.

Customer Analysis:

Customer segmentation and personalisation is a significant additional application for predictive analytics techniques. Businesses can identify various client segments and adjust their marketing tactics to meet the demands of each segment by evaluating customer data, such as demographics, preferences, and historical behaviors. To increase customer engagement and conversion rates, an e-commerce business might use predictive analytics techniques to generate personalized product recommendations for specific customers based on their browsing and purchase history.

Fraud Detection:

Identifying abnormalities and fraud requires the use of predictive analytics techniques. These technologies can find anomalous or suspicious actions that differ from the norm by examining patterns and previous data. For example, financial organizations might use these technologies to identify fraudulent transactions or activities, reducing possible losses and protecting the interests of their clients.

Comparative Data Utility:

Predictive analytics solutions provide a wide range of functionalities in terms of features and capacities. Users may clean, process, and combine data from multiple sources thanks to their complete data preparation capabilities. These tools frequently come with a sizable collection of statistical models and machine learning algorithms, allowing users to create prediction models that are customized to their unique requirements. They also provide comprehensive model evaluation metrics that let users evaluate the performance and correctness of their models.

Trend Detection:

Additionally, a lot of predictive analytics solutions include simple data visualization features. Users can successfully share findings, study data, and spot trends thanks to these representations. Businesses may better comprehend their data and readily communicate their results to stakeholders by visualizing complex data patterns.

Improved Decision Making:

Advanced tools for predictive analytics enable businesses to harness the power of data and make wise decisions. Their uses cut across a range of sectors, from industry and healthcare to retail and banking. These tools give businesses the ability to estimate future results, find hidden insights, and enhance their operations by utilizing sophisticated statistical algorithms and machine learning approaches. We will explore more into particular predictive analytics tools, their use cases, and the distinctive characteristics that make them valuable tools in the data analytics toolbox in the sections that follow. So let's start this wonderful voyage and investigate the world of tools for predictive analytics!

Examples of Popular Predictive Analytics Tools:

IBM SPSS Modeler:

SPSS Modeler is a comprehensive predictive analytics tool that offers a visual interface for data preparation, modeling, and evaluation. It provides a wide range of algorithms and techniques for predictive modeling and allows users to build and deploy models without extensive programming knowledge.

RapidMiner:

RapidMiner is an open-source predictive analytics platform that offers a user-friendly interface for data preparation, modeling, and evaluation. It supports various machine learning algorithms, data visualization, and automation capabilities.

Microsoft Azure Machine Learning: Azure Machine Learning is a cloud-based platform that enables users to build, deploy, and manage predictive analytics models. It provides a range of tools and algorithms, integration with other Microsoft services, and scalability for handling large datasets.

SAS Predictive Analytics:

SAS Predictive Analytics is a comprehensive suite of tools for advanced analytics and modeling. It offers a wide range of algorithms, data exploration and visualization capabilities, and model deployment options.

Python with Scikit-learn: Python, along with the Scikit-learn library, is a popular choice for predictive analytics. Scikit-learn provides a range of machine learning algorithms and tools for data preprocessing, model training, and evaluation.

Features and Capabilities of Predictive Analytics Tools

Data Preparation:

Predictive analytics tools offer features for data cleaning, transformation, and integration. They allow users to handle missing values, outliers, and format inconsistencies to ensure data quality.

Model Building:

These tools provide a range of algorithms and techniques for building predictive models, such as regression, classification, and clustering. They also offer parameter tuning options and model evaluation metrics to optimize model performance.

Data Visualization:

Predictive analytics tools often include data visualization capabilities to help users explore and understand data patterns and relationships. Visualizations aid in identifying trends, outliers, and insights that can drive decision-making.

Model Evaluation:

These tools offer methods for evaluating the performance of predictive models, such as accuracy, precision, recall, and F1 score. They also provide validation techniques, such as cross-validation and holdout testing, to assess model generalization.

Deployment and Integration:

Predictive analytics tools allow users to deploy models into production environments and integrate them with other systems or applications. This facilitates the use of predictive models in real-time decision-making scenarios.

Natural Language Processing Tools Uses Cases in Data Analytics

The world of Natural Language Processing (NLP) tools is a fascinating one, so welcome! We produce a tremendous amount of text data in the digital age from a variety of sources, including social media, websites, emails, and papers. NLP techniques give us the ability to comprehend, analyse, and glean useful insights from this textual data. We will examine the foundations of NLP tools, their uses, and the essential characteristics that make them so valuable in the field of data analytics in this chapter.

The subfield of artificial intelligence called "Natural Language Processing" (NLP) is concerned with how computers and human language interact. By processing, comprehending, and analyzing natural language data, NLP technologies enable computers to interpret and produce meaningful human language.

Text Classification and Sentiment Analysis:

Text classification and sentiment analysis are two of the main uses of NLP software. With the use of these tools, text files can be automatically categorized into predetermined groups, such as spam or non-spam emails, news subjects, client reviews, or feelings on social media. Businesses can obtain important insights into customer attitudes, product feedback, and brand impression by analyzing the sentiment conveyed in text data.

Information Extraction and Entity Recognition:

Information extraction and named entity recognition are two further critical applications of NLP systems. From unstructured text data, these technologies may automatically recognize and extract particular pieces of information like names, dates, locations, organizations, or product mentions. Tasks like news summarization, data mining, or consumer feedback analysis benefit greatly from this skill.

Machine Translation:

Another well-known use of NLP techniques is machine translation. By automatically translating text into languages, these tools lower obstacles to communication and promote cross-cultural understanding. Examples include well-known translation technologies that use NLP, such as Google Translate, to offer precise and effective translation services.

Virtual Assistance:

NLP tools are also essential for chatbots and virtual assistants. These tools enable interactive and intelligent discussions between humans and robots by processing and comprehending inputs in human language. NLP capabilities are used by virtual assistants like Siri, Alexa, or Google Assistant to comprehend user requests, deliver pertinent information, and carry out tasks like creating reminders, responding to inquiries, or managing smart home devices.

Tokenization:

NLP tools provide a wide range of functionalities in terms of features and skills. They consist of methods like tokenization, which allows for additional analysis by dissecting text into individual words or sentences. By assigning grammatical tags to words, parts-of-speech tagging aids in syntactic analysis and the comprehension of sentence structure. Named entity recognition locates and categorizes named entities—such as names of people, businesses, or places—within text data.

To ascertain the sentiment expressed in textual information, whether it is favorable, negative, or neutral, NLP systems also integrate sentiment analysis algorithms. They also include methods for extracting underlying topics from a group of texts, such as Latent Dirichlet Allocation (LDA) topic modeling techniques. These qualities make it possible for enterprises to effectively mine massive amounts of text data for insightful information.

NLP technologies are crucial in the field of data analytics because they enable us to uncover the important information that is concealed inside textual data. These techniques, which range from sentiment analysis and text classification to machine translation and chatbots, enable businesses to comprehend and engage with human language broadly. As we continue reading this chapter, we will examine several NLP tools, their uses, and the special qualities that make them essential in the toolbox for data analytics. So let's start this thrilling trip and go deeper into the interesting realm of Natural Language Processing (NLP) tools.

There are several powerful NLP tools available that are widely used in data analytics to extract insights from textual data. Let's explore a few prominent examples:

NLTK (Natural Language Toolkit):

NLTK is a popular Python library for NLP that provides a wide range of functionalities, including tokenization, stemming, lemmatization, part-of-speech tagging, and named entity recognition. It offers various corpora and lexicons for training and testing NLP models. NLTK is widely used in academic research, prototyping NLP applications, and building custom NLP solutions.

SpaCy:

SpaCy is another widely adopted Python library for NLP. It offers efficient and fast natural language processing capabilities, including tokenization, part-of-speech tagging, named entity recognition, and dependency parsing. SpaCy is known for its speed and ease of use, making it suitable for processing large volumes of text data. It also provides pre-trained models for various languages, allowing for easy integration into NLP pipelines.

Stanford NLP:

The Stanford NLP toolkit is a suite of NLP tools developed by the Stanford Natural Language Processing Group. It includes a range of NLP functionalities such as part-of-speech tagging, named entity recognition, sentiment analysis, coreference resolution, and parsing. The toolkit provides highly accurate models trained on large-scale annotated datasets. It is often used in research and academic projects for advanced NLP tasks.

Gensim:

Gensim is a Python library for topic modeling and document similarity analysis. It provides efficient implementations of algorithms like Latent Semantic Analysis (LSA), Latent Dirichlet Allocation (LDA), and Word2Vec. Gensim allows users to discover hidden topics within a collection of documents and extract semantic relationships between words. It is widely used for text clustering, document similarity analysis, and recommendation systems.

IBM Watson NLP:

IBM Watson offers a suite of powerful NLP tools and services through its Watson Natural Language

Understanding (NLU) platform. It provides functionalities like entity extraction, sentiment analysis, keyword extraction, and emotion detection. IBM Watson NLP leverages advanced machine learning models and is known for its accuracy and scalability. It is widely used in industries such as healthcare, finance, and customer service for analyzing unstructured text data.

Google Cloud Natural Language API:

Google Cloud Natural Language API is a cloud-based NLP service that provides a range of powerful capabilities, including entity recognition, sentiment analysis, content classification, and syntax analysis. It leverages Google's extensive language understanding models to extract valuable insights from text data. The API is user-friendly, scalable, and can be easily integrated into applications and workflows.

These are just a few examples of the many NLP tools available for data analytics. Each tool has its strengths and focuses on different aspects of NLP. The choice of the tool depends on the specific requirements of the project, the complexity of the tasks, and the volume of data to be processed. It's important to evaluate the features, performance, and ease of integration of each tool to select the most suitable one for a given NLP application in data analytics.

Text Mining and Sentiment Analysis with NLP Tools

Text mining and sentiment analysis are powerful applications of NLP tools that allow us to extract valuable insights and understand the sentiment expressed in textual data. Let's delve into these topics and explore how NLP tools facilitate text mining and sentiment analysis.

Text Mining:

Text mining, also known as text analytics, involves extracting useful information and patterns from unstructured text data. NLP tools play a crucial role in this process by providing various techniques and functionalities.

Tokenization:

NLP tools tokenize text by breaking it down into individual words or sentences. This helps in further analysis and understanding the structure of the text.

Part-of-speech (POS) tagging:

POS tagging assigns grammatical tags to words in a sentence, such as nouns, verbs, adjectives, or adverbs. This enables the identification of the role each word plays in the sentence, which is useful for syntactic analysis and understanding the context.

Named Entity Recognition (NER):

NER is the process of identifying and classifying named entities, such as names of people, organizations, locations, or product mentions, within the text. NLP tools use machine learning algorithms to automatically recognize and extract these entities, facilitating information extraction and organization.

Sentiment Analysis:

Sentiment analysis, also known as opinion mining, aims to determine the sentiment expressed in textual data, whether it is positive, negative, or neutral. NLP tools provide several techniques and features to perform sentiment analysis effectively.

Lexicon-Based Approaches:

NLP tools use pre-built sentiment lexicons or dictionaries that associate words with their sentiment polarity (positive, negative, or neutral). By analyzing the sentiment polarity of individual words in a sentence, the overall sentiment of the text can be determined.

Machine Learning-based approaches:

NLP tools employ machine learning algorithms, such as Naive Bayes, Support Vector Machines, or Recurrent Neural Networks, to train sentiment classification models. These models learn from labeled training data and can accurately classify text into positive, negative, or neutral sentiment categories.

Aspect-Based Sentiment Analysis:

NLP tools can also perform aspect-based sentiment analysis, where they identify and analyze the sentiment associated with specific aspects or features of a product, service, or topic. This enables a more fine-grained understanding of sentiment and helps businesses identify areas of improvement or strength.

Use Cases and Examples:

Text mining and sentiment analysis with NLP tools find applications in various industries and domains:

Customer feedback analysis:

NLP tools can analyze customer reviews, social media comments, or surveys to understand customer sentiment towards a product or service. This helps businesses identify trends, gauge customer satisfaction, and make data-driven decisions to improve their offerings.

Brand monitoring:

NLP tools can monitor online discussions, social media mentions, or news articles related to a brand. By analyzing the sentiment associated with these mentions, businesses can track brand perception, identify potential issues or crises, and take proactive measures to manage their reputation.

Market research:

NLP tools enable efficient analysis of market research reports, industry trends, or competitor analysis. By extracting key insights from these textual sources, businesses can identify market opportunities, consumer preferences, and emerging trends.

Financial sentiment analysis:

NLP tools can analyze news articles, social media posts, and financial reports to gauge the sentiment towards specific companies, stocks, or financial instruments. This information helps investors and financial institutions make informed decisions about investments or market trends.

Customer support and chatbots:

NLP tools power chatbot systems that can understand and respond to customer queries, providing personalized assistance. Sentiment analysis helps in identifying customer frustration or satisfaction, allowing businesses to provide timely and appropriate responses.

NLP tools like NLTK, SpaCy, IBM Watson NLU, or Google Cloud Natural Language API provide robust text mining and sentiment analysis capabilities. They offer pre-built models, APIs, and customizable options to suit different use cases and industry requirements. By leveraging these tools, businesses can extract valuable insights, understand customer sentiment, and make data-driven decisions to enhance their products, services, and overall customer experience.

Machine Learning Platforms for Data Analysis

In order to harness the power of machine learning algorithms and create predictive models at scale, machine learning platforms have become crucial tools for organizations. These platforms offer a comprehensive collection of tools, libraries, and frameworks that simplify the creation, testing, and deployment of machine learning models from start to finish. We will examine use cases, examples, and the procedure for developing and deploying machine learning models with well-known machine learning platforms in this section.

Use cases for machine learning platforms

These platforms are used in a variety of industries and fields. Here are some well-known use cases:

Fraud Detection:

Machine learning platforms can be used to build models that examine trends and outliers in financial transactions to spot fraudulent behavior. These models can identify fraudulent activity in real-time and learn from historical data, assisting organizations in reducing financial losses.

Customer Churn Prediction:

Machine learning platforms make it possible to create predictive models that pinpoint clients who are at risk of canceling their subscriptions or churning. Organizations can take proactive steps to keep customers and improve their marketing strategies by analyzing customer behavior and patterns.

Systems for making recommendations:

Machine learning platforms are used to create systems for making recommendations that offer users personalized suggestions based on their preferences and behavior. To improve user experience and raise engagement, these systems are widely used in e-commerce, streaming services, and content platforms.

Predictive Maintenance:

Organizations can create models that foretell equipment failures or require maintenance based on sensor data and previous maintenance records using machine learning platforms. This enhances operational effectiveness, lowers downtime, and optimizes maintenance schedules.

Medical Imaging and Digital Health Records:

Medical imaging and electronic health records are two examples of the types of medical data that machine learning platforms can be used to analyze to create models that can help with disease diagnosis, prognosis, and treatment planning. These models can help medical professionals make decisions that are more timely and accurate.

Popular machine learning platform illustrations

TensorFlow:

TensorFlow is an open-source machine learning platform created by Google that offers a complete ecosystem for creating and deploying machine learning models. It provides a flexible framework and high-level API (Keras) for creating neural networks and other machine learning algorithms. TensorFlow has grown in popularity due to its adaptability and scalability and supports distributed computing.

PyTorch:

Another open-source machine learning platform is PyTorch, which is renowned for its user-friendliness and dynamic computational graph. It offers a Python-based ecosystem that gives researchers and developers the flexibility to create and train neural networks. In both research and production settings, PyTorch is frequently used.

Microsoft Azure:

Microsoft Azure Machine Learning is a cloud-based platform for machine learning that provides a variety of tools and services for creating, honing, and deploying machine learning models. Additionally, it offers seamless integration with other Azure services, pre-built AI models, automated machine learning, and a collaborative environment.

Amazon SageMaker:

Amazon SageMaker: Provided by Amazon Web Services (AWS), Amazon SageMaker is a fully managed machine learning platform. For creating, honing, and deploying machine learning models, it offers a scalable infrastructure and an extensive set of tools. SageMaker streamlines the entire machine learning workflow and supports a number of well-liked machine learning frameworks.

Using ML platforms to build and deploy machine learning models

ML platforms provide a streamlined process for building and deploying machine learning models. The general steps are as follows:

Gathering and preprocessing the data needed for the model's training constitutes the first step in the process. This entails preparing the data, handling missing values, and formatting it appropriately.Model development is made possible by a variety of algorithms and libraries offered by machine learning platforms. To enhance model performance, users can configure hyperparameters and select the appropriate algorithms.

Model Evaluation:

Using different evaluation metrics and techniques, machine learning platforms allow users to assess the trained models. This makes it easier to evaluate the model's performance and make the necessary adjustments.

Deployment:

After the model has been trained and assessed, machine learning platforms offer tools for deploying the model into real-world settings. This might entail integrating the model with other systems or exporting it as a deployable artifact.

Monitoring and iteration:

To track the model's performance in real-time, machine learning platforms frequently provide monitoring and feedback mechanisms. This enables organizations to iterate and improve the model over time in response to fresh data and changing requirements.

In conclusion, machine learning platforms are essential for enabling businesses to harness the power of machine learning and create complex predictive models. They simplify the process of developing and deploying machine learning models and offer a wide range of use cases, from fraud detection to recommendation systems. Organizations can unleash the potential of machine learning and spur innovation in their specific fields by utilizing well-known platforms like TensorFlow, PyTorch,

Microsoft Azure Machine Learning, and Amazon SageMaker.

Data Visualization and Business Intelligence (BI) Tools

Organizations need data visualization and business intelligence (BI) tools in order to understand their data and make wise business decisions. These tools enable the visual representation of data in the form of interactive dashboards, graphs, and charts, making it simpler to comprehend complex data and spot patterns or trends. In this section, we'll look at use cases, popular tool examples, and how to use visualization tools to create interactive dashboards and reports.

Use cases for BI and data visualization tools include:

Tools for business intelligence and data visualization are used in many different sectors and fields. Here are some well-known use cases:

Sales Analysis, Customer Behavior and Marketing:

Data visualization tools can be used by businesses to analyze sales data, consumer behavior, and marketing campaigns. Organizations can pinpoint sales trends, customer preferences, and improve marketing strategies by visually representing the data.

Budgeting, forecasting, and other aspects of financial analysis can be aided by data visualization and business intelligence (BI) tools. Financial analysts can examine financial data interactively, spot anomalies, and gain insights to help them make decisions.

Supply Chain Management:

Organizations can analyze and improve their supply chain operations with the aid of visualization tools. Businesses can spot bottlenecks, increase productivity, and cut costs by visualizing key supply chain metrics like inventory levels, order fulfillment, and transportation costs.

Analyzing Customer Data:

Analyzing customer data, including demographics, purchase history, and customer satisfaction metrics, is made possible by data visualization tools. Organizations can segment customers, learn about their preferences, and tailor marketing campaigns or customer experiences by visualizing this information.

Popular Data Visualization and BI Tools

Tableau:

Tableau is a popular BI and data visualization tool that enables users to build interactive dashboards, reports, and visualizations. It supports different data sources, has a drag-and-drop interface, and offers a wide range of charting options. Tableau is a popular option for data analysis and visualization because of its user-friendly interface and robust features.

Microsoft Power BI:

Microsoft Power BI is a tool for business analytics that offers interactive dashboards and visualizations. Users can create interactive reports, connect to numerous data sources, and share insights with others. A variety of features are available in Power BI for advanced analytics, collaboration, and data exploration.

QlikView:

Users can visually explore and analyze data using QlikView, a self-service BI and data visualization platform. It provides an associative data model that enables users to explore and navigate data relationships in real time. The interactive and associative features of QlikView make it suitable for data exploration and discovery.

Google Data Studio:

Users can create interactive dashboards and reports using Google Data Studio, a free tool for data visualization. It provides integration with a number of data sources, including BigQuery, Google Analytics, and Google Sheets. A straightforward and user-friendly interface is provided by Data Studio for creating visually appealing reports and sharing them with others.

Utilizing visualization tools to create interactive dashboards and reports:

Data exploration and analysis are made easier by interactive dashboards and reports made with the help of visualization tools. The following steps can be used to create interactive dashboards and reports:

Gathering and preparing the data for visualization is the first step. This could entail cleansing the data, formatting it appropriately, and connecting to data sources.

Users can select from a variety of chart types, including bar charts, line charts, scatter plots, and maps, to visually represent the data after it has been prepared. In order to improve the dashboard's or report's aesthetics and clarity, users can also customize the visual components, such as the colors, labels, and titles.

Interactive Features: Interactive features in visualization tools, such as drill-downs, tooltips, and filters, let users delve deeper into the data. Users can define interactions and behaviors based on their own interactions, which allows them to interact with the visualizations in a dynamic way.

Dashboard Construction: Visualization tools offer a canvas so that users can put various visualizations together to create a single dashboard or report. For effective storytelling, users can arrange the visualizations, add text or annotations, and organize the information in a logical flow.

Collaboration and Sharing: After the interactive dashboard or report is created, users can invite others within the company to use it. Collaboration and knowledge sharing are facilitated by visualization tools' frequent options to publish dashboards or reports on the web or embed them in other applications.

In conclusion, BI tools and data visualization play a critical role in assisting organizations in drawing conclusions from their data and making data-driven decisions. Powerful features and capabilities are offered by well-known tools like Tableau, Microsoft Power BI, QlikView, and Google Data Studio to create interactive dashboards and reports. These tools enable businesses to explore and analyze data visually, spot trends and patterns, and effectively share insights.

Automated Data Preparation Tools

As they streamlined and sped up the process of cleaning, transforming, and preparing data for analysis, automated data preparation tools have become essential in the field of data analytics. To address various data challenges like missing values, outliers, inconsistent formats, and data integration, these tools make use of cutting-edge algorithms and techniques. In this section, we'll look at some of the applications for automated data preparation tools, give some examples of well-known ones, and talk about how these tools can speed up the data cleansing and transformation procedures.

Automated Data Preparation Tools' Use Cases

Data Cleaning:

Data cleaning tasks, such as locating and managing missing values, outliers, duplicates, and inconsistent data formats, are best handled by automated data preparation tools. These tools can save time and effort by automatically identifying appropriate actions and suggesting them, such as adding missing values or eliminating outliers.

Data Integration:

Automated data preparation tools can help with data integration tasks when working with data from multiple sources or in different formats. They can handle data transformations, automatically align and merge datasets, and fix inconsistencies to make sure that data from various sources can be used for joint analysis.

To increase the predictive ability of machine learning models, feature engineering involves creating new variables or altering existing ones. The feature engineering process is made easier by the functionality provided by automated data preparation tools, which can automatically create new features based on data patterns, carry out mathematical operations, or encode categorical variables.

Data Transformation:

Automated data preparation tools provide functionalities for scaling, normalizing, or standardizing variables, enabling effective data transformation. These tools can handle intricate transformations like polynomial expansion and logarithmic scaling, ensuring that data is in a format that is suitable for analysis.

Tools for Automating Data Preparation

DataRobot:

DataRobot is a well-known platform for automated machine learning that includes automated data preparation features. It offers tools for data integration, transformation, and cleaning, enabling users to fully automate the data preparation process before creating predictive models.

Trifacta:

Trifacta is a platform for data preparation that uses interactive visualizations and machine learning to automate data cleaning and transformation tasks. It provides simple tools for handling anomalies, filling in missing values, and generating new variables based on patterns in the data.

Alteryx:

An extensive analytics platform with automated data preparation tools is called Alteryx. It offers a visual user interface for tasks involving data integration, transformation, and cleaning. Users of Alteryx can create data pipelines to automate data preparation and guarantee analysis-ready data.

RapidMiner:

RapidMiner is a free and open-source platform for data science that provides automated data preparation features. For data cleaning, transformation, and integration, it offers a variety of operators and workflows. Users can concentrate on gaining insights because RapidMiner makes the process of preparing data for analysis more straightforward.

Using automated tools to streamline data transformation and cleaning

Through a variety of methods and features, automated data preparation tools streamline the processes of data cleaning and transformation. These tools make data preparation simpler and better in the following ways:

Data Profiling:

Tools for automated data preparation frequently have data profiling features that give a general overview of the distributions, statistics, and quality of the data. This aids users in comprehending the properties of the data and in spotting any potential problems that call for cleaning or transformation.

Data Imputation:

One of the most important steps in data preparation is handling missing values. Automated tools provide clever algorithms that extrapolate missing values from data patterns. To accurately fill in missing values, they can, for instance, use mean imputation, regression imputation, or imputation based on similar records.

Outlier Detection:

Outliers have a big impact on the analysis's findings. To find outliers and offer options for handling them, such as removing outliers or transforming the data to lessen their impact, automated tools use statistical techniques or machine learning algorithms.

Data Integration and Transformation:

By automatically identifying common variables and handling inconsistencies in formats or structures, automated tools streamline the process of integrating data from various sources. In order to transform variables into appropriate formats for analysis, they also offer pre-built transformations or custom transformation options.

Data Validation:

To guarantee data quality and compliance with predefined rules or constraints, automated data preparation tools frequently include validation features. This aids in locating problems with data integrity and preserving the consistency and accuracy of the data.

In summary, automated data preparation tools are essential for improving and streamlining the data cleaning and transformation procedures in data analytics. For tasks involving data integration, transformation, and feature engineering, they provide effective solutions. The well-known tools DataRobot, Trifacta, Alteryx, and RapidMiner are a few examples. Organizations can save time, enhance data quality, and concentrate on gaining insightful information from their data by utilizing these tools.

Deep Learning Frameworks

The ability to create and use sophisticated deep neural networks has revolutionized the field of artificial intelligence thanks to deep learning frameworks. The implementation, training, and evaluation of deep learning models are made easier by the comprehensive set of tools, libraries, and APIs that these frameworks offer. This section will examine the applications of deep learning frameworks, give illustrations of well-known frameworks, and go over how to use them for complex data analysis.

Deep Learning Framework Use Cases

Image Detection:

Image recognition tasks like object detection, image classification, and semantic segmentation have all seen extensive use of deep learning frameworks. These frameworks are remarkably accurate at identifying objects and recognizing complex visual patterns because they can automatically learn intricate patterns and features from images.

Several image recognition applications, such as self-driving cars, medical imaging diagnosis, and facial recognition systems, have used the well-known deep learning framework TensorFlow.

Natural Language Processing (NLP):

By enabling the creation of models that comprehend and produce human language, deep learning frameworks have significantly advanced the field of NLP. They have been applied to projects like chatbot development, sentiment analysis, language translation, and text generation.

Popular deep learning framework PyTorch has been used for NLP tasks, such as question-answering systems, language modeling, and machine translation systems.

Deep learning frameworks have been instrumental in improving the precision and usability of voice-controlled systems in speech recognition applications. They make it possible to create models that can understand spoken commands, convert speech to text, and transcribe it.

As an illustration, consider Keras, a user-friendly deep learning framework that has been applied to a number of speech recognition applications, including voice assistants like Siri and Google Assistant.

Illustrations of Well-Known Deep Learning Frameworks

TensorFlow:

TensorFlow, one of the most popular deep learning frameworks, was created by Google. A complete ecosystem is offered for developing and deploying deep learning models. Numerous neural network architectures are supported by TensorFlow, which also provides high-level APIs like Keras for quick model development.

PyTorch:

Another well-liked deep learning framework is PyTorch, which is renowned for its ability to create dynamic computational graphs. It offers a versatile and simple programming interface that makes experimenting with intricate models simpler. Due to its simplicity of use and extensive support for tasks geared toward conducting research, PyTorch is widely used in academia and industry.

Keras:

A high-level deep learning framework called Keras sits on top of frameworks like TensorFlow and Theano. It provides a straightforward and user-friendly interface, which makes it a great option for beginners. Keras supports CPU and GPU acceleration and offers simple building blocks for creating neural networks.

Using deep learning models to implement complex data analysis:

The tools and capabilities needed to implement complex models for data analysis tasks are provided by deep learning frameworks. Implementing deep learning models involves the following steps:

Data preprocessing:

It is crucial to perform data preprocessing before training a deep learning model. Data normalization, handling missing values, and dividing the data into training and testing sets are a few examples of tasks that may be involved. To effectively handle these tasks, deep learning frameworks provide functionalities and preprocessing tools.

Model Architecture: Deep learning frameworks let users specify how their neural networks are structured. This includes describing the quantity, kind, and connectivity of the layers (convolutional, recurrent, etc.). APIs and libraries are available for creating unique architectures or using pre-trained models in frameworks like TensorFlow and PyTorch.

Model Training:

Deep learning frameworks offer methods for putting the available data to use in neural network training. In order to do this, training data must be fed into the model, loss or error must be calculated, and backpropagation must be used to update the model's parameters. Frameworks provide utilities and optimization algorithms to speed up the training process.

Model Evaluation:

Deep learning frameworks enable users to assess the performance of their models on untrained data after training. They offer evaluation metrics for the task at hand-specific accuracy, precision, recall, and other metrics. This aids in evaluating the model's performance and making any necessary corrections.

To sum up, deep learning frameworks have made it possible to create sophisticated neural network models for a variety of data analysis tasks. Popular deep learning frameworks that provide extensive functionalities and support include TensorFlow, PyTorch, and Keras. These frameworks are used in a variety of fields, including speech recognition, natural language processing, and image recognition. These frameworks enable researchers and data analysts to quickly and effectively implement robust deep learning models for challenging data analysis tasks.

Data Mining and Pattern Recognition Tools

Tools for data mining and pattern recognition are crucial parts of data analytics because they make it possible to find hidden patterns, trends, and insights in huge datasets. Organizations can use these tools to extract useful information from unstructured data and make data-driven decisions because they use sophisticated algorithms and techniques to do so. In this section, we'll examine the applications of data mining and pattern recognition tools, give examples of well-known ones, and talk about how these techniques reveal hidden patterns and insights.

Use Cases of Data Mining And Pattern Recognition Software

Customer Segmentation:

Based on their behavior, preferences, and demographics, customers can be divided into groups. These tools can identify distinct customer groups with a shared set of traits by analyzing customer data. Businesses can customize their marketing strategies, offer more specialized product recommendations, and increase customer satisfaction thanks to this segmentation. For instance, the program "IBM SPSS Modeler" offers clustering algorithms that let companies divide their clientele into various groups based on how they behave when making purchases. This enables them to focus their marketing efforts on particular clientele groups.

Fraud Detection:

By examining patterns and anomalies in financial transactions, insurance claims, or online activities, data mining tools play a key role in identifying fraudulent activities. These tools help organizations stop financial losses and safeguard against fraud by identifying suspicious patterns that might indicate fraudulent behavior.

"RapidMiner," which offers a variety of machine learning algorithms to find patterns and anomalies in large datasets, is one well-liked tool for fraud detection. It can assist insurance companies in identifying potentially fraudulent claims or financial institutions in detecting fraudulent transactions.

Market Basket Analysis:

Based on customer purchase behavior, market basket analysis is a technique used to identify relationships and associations between products. With the help of data mining tools, businesses can understand customer preferences, improve product placement, and implement targeted cross-selling or upselling strategies by identifying frequently occurring items in transactional data.

Market basket analysis can be carried out on transactional data using the association rule mining algorithms provided by the "Weka" tool. It can discover connections between products in a retail dataset, such as the likelihood that customers who buy diapers will also buy baby wipes.

Tools for Pattern Recognition And Data Mining

RapidMiner:

RapidMiner is a well-known data mining tool that offers a variety of functionalities for data analysis and predictive modeling. It allows for the creation and deployment of data mining workflows visually, making it usable by both technical and non-technical users. For classification, regression, clustering, and association rule mining, RapidMiner supports a number of algorithms.

KNIME:

KNIME is an open-source data analytics platform that offers a graphical user interface for creating data pipelines and carrying out data mining operations. It provides a wide range of tools and methods for preprocessing, modeling, and visualization of data. KNIME is appropriate for a variety of data mining applications because it offers extensive support for machine learning and statistical analysis.

SAS Enterprise Miner is a thorough data mining tool with sophisticated analytics features for predictive modeling, text mining, and optimization. A variety of statistical and machine learning algorithms are available, along with a visual user interface. For enterprise-level data mining projects, SAS Enterprise Miner is a good choice because of its scalability and capacity for handling large datasets.

Using mining tools to elucidate hidden patterns and insights

Tools for data mining and pattern recognition use a variety of methods to find hidden patterns and insights in data. These methods consist of:

Association Rule Mining:

The technique of "association rule mining" identifies connections and associations between objects in a dataset. It can, for instance, tell you whether customers who buy product A are also likely to buy product B.

Clustering:

Based on the attributes of the data points, clustering algorithms group related data points together. By assisting in the discovery of natural groupings within the data, this enables businesses to comprehend customer segments or spot trends in consumer behavior.

Anomaly Detection:

Identifying data points or patterns that significantly deviate from the norm is known as anomaly detection. This helps identify fraud, atypical occurrences, or data outliers.

These methods can be used by data mining tools to uncover important information that might not be visible through manual data exploration. These insights can then be applied to inform decision-making, enhance business operations, or acquire a market advantage.

In conclusion, data analytics tools like pattern recognition and data mining are extremely useful. They help businesses find hidden patterns and insights within massive datasets, enabling them to make better decisions. These tools have a variety of applications, including market basket analysis, fraud detection, and customer segmentation. RapidMiner, KNIME, and SAS Enterprise Miner are a few well-known examples. Businesses can gain insightful information and make data-driven decisions to stay competitive in today's data-driven world by utilizing the capabilities of these tools.

Automated Machine Learning (AutoML) Tools

By streamlining and automating numerous tasks involved in developing and deploying machine learning models, automated machine learning (AutoML) tools have revolutionized the field of machine learning. By enabling users with little programming or data science experience to take advantage of the power of machine learning algorithms, these tools seek to democratize machine learning. This section will examine the applications of AutoML tools, offer illustrations of well-known tools, and go over how they streamline the machine learning procedure.

Use Cases for Automl Tools

Image Classification:

Without the need for manual feature engineering or difficult algorithm selection, image classification models can be built using autoML tools. The preprocessing of data, the choice of suitable algorithms, and the improvement of model performance are all automated by these tools. They are especially helpful in sectors like manufacturing, retail, and the healthcare sector where image analysis is essential.

Using their own labeled data, users can train their own image classification models using Google Cloud AutoML Vision, for instance. This enables companies to create image recognition systems powered by AI that are customized for their unique requirements.

Predictive Analytics:

The construction of predictive models, including tasks like data preprocessing, feature selection, algorithm selection, and hyperparameter tuning, can be automated using autoML tools. This makes it possible for domain specialists and business analysts to create precise predictive models without having a deep understanding of machine learning methods.

The popular AutoML tool from H2O.ai automates the creation and selection of the best machine learning models for predictive analytics from beginning to end. It performs automated feature engineering and model selection in addition to offering a wide range of algorithms.

Natural Language Processing (NLP):

AutoML tools can make the process of creating NLP models, including tasks like named entity recognition, sentiment analysis, and text classification, simpler. By automating tokenization, feature extraction, and model training, these tools free up users to concentrate on the NLP applications' domain-specific features.

The Ludwig AutoML framework is one illustration, which enables users to train NLP models with little to no coding. It handles difficult tasks like selecting suitable model architectures and preprocessing textual data as well as providing a high-level API for building models.

Illustrations of Well-Known Automl Tools

Google Cloud AutoML:

Google Cloud AutoML is a collection of AutoML tools that spans a number of areas, including tabular data, natural language processing, and vision. Without requiring in-depth knowledge of machine learning algorithms, it offers a user-friendly interface for training and deploying machine learning models.

H2O.ai's AutoML:

A comprehensive AutoML platform that supports a variety of machine learning tasks, H2O.ai's AutoML. Data preprocessing, model selection, and hyperparameter tuning are all automated, making it simple for non-experts to use.

DataRobot:

DataRobot is a top AutoML platform that aims to make machine learning accessible to all users. For creating and deploying machine learning models across numerous domains and industries, it offers an easy-to-use interface. By automating many steps in the machine learning process, DataRobot's platform frees users to concentrate on business insights rather than technical implementation.

Using automated tools to streamline the machine learning process:

By automating laborious and complicated tasks, autoML tools streamline the machine learning process and free up users to concentrate on making higher-level decisions and deriving insights from the models. The following advantages are offered by these tools:

Automated Feature Engineering:

AutoML tools generate and select pertinent features from the raw data automatically, automating the feature engineering process. This eliminates the need for labor- and error-intensive manual feature engineering.

AutoML tools choose the best machine learning algorithms for a given task and tune their hyperparameters. This is known as algorithm selection. Users are spared the effort of trying out various algorithm and parameter combinations because the tools will automatically select the model with the best performance.

Model Interpretability:

Some AutoML tools give users explanations or insights into how the model makes decisions, allowing them to comprehend and interpret the model's predictions. In fields like healthcare and finance, where interpretability and transparency are essential, this is especially significant.

In conclusion, AutoML tools have become effective tools for streamlining the machine learning process and opening it up to a larger user base. They provide a variety of use cases, including NLP applications, image classification, and predictive analytics. Popular examples include DataRobot, H2O.ai's AutoML, and Google Cloud AutoML. Businesses can gain from automated feature engineering, algorithm selection, and model tuning by utilizing these tools, which will result in quicker and more accurate predictions and insights.

Cognitive Analytic Tools

Utilizing artificial intelligence (AI) technologies, cognitive analytics tools analyze complex data patterns and behavior, providing organizations with insightful data on which to base decisions. To analyze and interpret data in a manner akin to a human, these tools combine advanced analytics methods with NLP, machine learning, and cognitive computing. We will discuss how organizations can use cognitive analytics tools to understand complex data patterns and behavior in this section, go over some examples of well-known tools, and explore the use cases for these tools.

Use Cases of Cognitive Analytics Tools

Customer Experience Analysis:

To better understand customer sentiment, preferences, and behavior, cognitive analytics tools can analyze customer interactions, such as emails, chat logs, and social media posts. Organizations can personalize their offerings, identify emerging trends, and enhance the customer experience with the aid of this analysis.

For instance, IBM Watson Customer Experience Analytics analyzes customer feedback from a variety of channels using AI-powered cognitive analytics and offers useful insights to improve customer satisfaction and loyalty.

Fraud detection:

To find fraudulent activities, cognitive analytics tools can find patterns and anomalies in massive amounts of data. These tools can identify unusual behaviors and patterns suggestive of fraud by examining historical data and current transactions.

The SAS Fraud Framework is one illustration of a tool that uses cognitive analytics techniques to identify fraud in a variety of channels, including banking, insurance, and retail. It combines machine learning algorithms and rule-based models to spot suspicious behavior and stop fraudulent transactions.

Risk Analysis:

By examining structured and unstructured data from various sources, cognitive analytics tools assist organizations in assessing and managing risks. These tools allow organizations to make data-driven decisions and reduce risks by spotting patterns, correlations, and anomalies in data.

For instance, RiskLens is a cognitive analytics platform that quantifies and ranks cyber risks using AI and advanced analytics. In order to give organizations insights for risk management and mitigation, it analyzes data pertaining to vulnerabilities, threats, and potential impacts.

Tools for Cognitive Analytics

In order to help users glean insights from both structured and unstructured data, IBM Watson Analytics is a cognitive analytics tool that combines AI, machine learning, and NLP. Data visualization, natural language querying, and predictive analytics are just a few of the features it offers.

Microsoft Azure Cognitive Services:

A set of AI-powered APIs and tools for cognitive analytics are offered by Microsoft Azure Cognitive Services. These services, which enable businesses to create intelligent applications, include sentiment analysis, language comprehension, image recognition, and speech recognition.

Salesforce Einstein Analytics:

To analyze customer data and deliver useful insights, Salesforce Einstein Analytics makes use of AI and machine learning. Users can find patterns and make data-driven decisions thanks to features like predictive modeling, automated data preparation, and natural language queries.

Using AI to comprehend intricate data patterns and behavior

To comprehend complex data patterns and behavior that may be challenging to identify through conventional data analysis methods, cognitive analytics tools make use of AI technologies. To uncover important patterns and insights, these tools can analyze enormous amounts of structured and unstructured data, including text, images, and audio.

These tools can find correlations, find anomalies, and predict the future using historical data by utilizing AI algorithms. They can extract meaning from unstructured data sources like social media posts, customer reviews, or research articles by spotting hidden patterns, comprehending human language, and doing so.

As a result, businesses are able to comprehend their clients, markets, and operations better, which helps them make better decisions and predict the future with greater accuracy.

To sum up, cognitive analytics tools are potent tools in the data analytics world. They make it possible for businesses to use AI technologies to comprehend intricate data patterns and behavior. These tools can be used for a variety of purposes, including risk analysis, fraud detection, and customer experience analysis. Examples that are frequently used include Salesforce Einstein Analytics, Microsoft Azure Cognitive Services, and IBM Watson Analytics. Utilizing these tools, businesses can gain insightful knowledge from their data and take well-informed decisions that will improve their bottom line.

Real Time Analytics Tools

In today's data-driven world, real-time analytics tools are essential because they allow organizations to process and analyze streaming data in real-time, delivering quick insights and useful information. These tools assist organizations in keeping track of, analyzing, and responding to events in real time, enabling them to make data-driven decisions and seize new opportunities. In this section, we will examine real-time analytics tool use cases, give examples of well-known tools, and go over how these tools make it possible to process and analyze streaming data in order to gain quick insights.

Real-Time Analytics Tools Use Cases

Financial Services:

The financial services sector makes extensive use of real-time analytics tools to track market data, spot anomalies, and execute trades immediately. These tools give traders and analysts the ability to adapt to market changes quickly and improve investment plans. As an illustration, Bloomberg Terminal offers real-time financial data and analytics, enabling users to keep track of news and market trends as well as conduct real-time analysis for trading purposes.

E-commerce:

To track customer behavior, improve pricing strategies, and customize the customer experience, e-commerce businesses must have access to real-time analytics tools. With the help of these tools, businesses can analyze customer data in real-time and provide specialized product recommendations or promotions.

Organizations can capture, process, and analyze streaming data in real-time using Amazon Kinesis, a real-time analytics tool offered by Amazon Web Services (AWS). Businesses are able to learn more about customer behavior and act right away to improve the shopping experience.

Internet of Things (IoT):

With the proliferation of IoT devices, real-time analytics tools are used to process and analyze data generated by these devices in real-time. Based on real-time insights, organizations can track device performance, spot anomalies, and take immediate action.

IoT applications use Splunk, a well-known real-time analytics platform, to gather and analyze machine data in real-time. It aids businesses in pattern recognition, operational efficiency optimization, and monitoring and management of IoT devices.

Illustrations of Real-Time Analytics Software

Apache Kafka:

A distributed streaming platform called Apache Kafka enables businesses to ingest, process, and analyze real-time data streams. Because it offers fault-tolerant, high-throughput messaging, it can be used for real-time analytics use cases.

Google Cloud Pub/Sub:

Organizations can publish and subscribe to real-time data streams using the messaging service Google Cloud Pub/Sub. It offers scalable and trustworthy data ingestion and delivery, supporting real-time analytics use cases.

Microsoft Azure Stream Analytics:

Microsoft Azure offers a real-time analytics service called Azure Stream Analytics. Organizations can use it to analyze streaming data from a variety of sources, like IoT devices or social media streams, and gain insightful knowledge immediately.

Streaming data processing and analysis for quick insights:

Organizations can process and analyze streaming data as it comes in with real-time analytics tools, giving them immediate insights and enabling them to take prompt action. To manage the constant flow of data, these tools frequently use techniques like stream processing and complex event processing (CEP).

Real-time processing of data streams is made possible by stream processing frameworks like Apache Flink and Apache Spark Streaming. This enables businesses to perform various data transformations, aggregations, and calculations on the data as it flows. They are able to gain insights and make decisions instantly as a result.

Esper and TIBCO StreamBase are examples of complex event processing (CEP) platforms that can handle and analyze large-scale event streams in real-time. As patterns, correlations, and anomalies are found in the data streams, these tools can take appropriate action or send out alerts when certain events take place.

With the aid of these utilities, organizations are able to identify critical events and react to them, keep an eye on key performance indicators (KPIs) in real-time, and automate business procedures using real-time insights.

In conclusion, organizations that want to use streaming data for quick insights and decisions must now have access to real-time analytics tools. They offer features like real-time data ingestion, processing, and analysis and find use in a variety of industries, including finance, e-commerce, and IoT. These tools give organizations a competitive edge, allow them to take advantage of emerging opportunities in today's fast-paced business environment, and can process and analyze data as it flows.

Key Considerations When Selecting AI Tools

There are several important factors to keep in mind when choosing AI tools for your company. These factors will make it easier for you to select the tools that are appropriate for your unique needs and objectives. The following are some crucial things to think about:

Business Objectives:

To begin, list your company's goals and the particular issues you hope to use AI to address. You can focus on the AI tools that are most appropriate for your needs by being aware of your goals.

Data Requirements:

Take into account the kind and amount of data you already have as well as the data needs of the AI tools. Make sure the tools are capable of handling your data volume and the data sources and formats you use.

Model Compatibilty:

Examine the AI tools' compatibility and integration with your current infrastructure and systems. To ensure seamless integration into your current technology stack, take into account elements like compatibility with your data storage platforms, APIs, and programming languages.

Capacity of the Tool:

Determine the AI tools' s capacity for scaling as your data and workload increase. Take into account elements like computing power in parallel, data handling capacity, and processing speed.

Ease of Use:

Consider how user-friendly the AI tools are. Look for tools that have user-friendly interfaces, clear instructions, and ample support. Your team will be able to quickly learn and use the technology thanks to user-friendly tools.

Flexibility and Customization:

Evaluate the degree of flexibility and customization that the AI tools provide. Find out if you can modify the tools to meet your unique needs and if they offer the flexibility you need to respond to shifting business requirements.

Model Interpretability and Explainability:

Understanding the justification behind AI-generated insights is essential in some industries, such as finance or healthcare. To ensure compliance and establish trust, take into account tools that provide transparency, interpretability, and explainability of their models.

Reputation and Support of the Developers:

Look into the standing and track record of the developers of AI tools. Look for vendors who have a good track record, many satisfied clients, and responsive customer service. Take into account elements like the vendor's industry expertise and dedication to ongoing product development and support.

Level of Security:

Examine the security measures that the AI tools have put in place to safeguard sensitive data. Make sure the tools have strong security components, such as encryption and access controls, and that they adhere to applicable data protection regulations.

Cost Considerations:

Lastly, think about how much the AI tools will cost, taking into account any licensing fees, maintenance costs, and possible scalability costs. Determine whether the tools are within your budget by evaluating the value they offer in relation to their price.

Before choosing one, it's critical to carefully assess and contrast various AI tools based on these factors. Consider conducting proof-of-concept initiatives or pilot studies as well to evaluate how well the tools function in your particular use case. By carefully taking into account these variables, you can choose AI tools that support your corporate goals and position yourself for success when implementing AI technologies.

This book would guide you to begin your journey from the scratch as a data analyst. I wish you good luck in this enterprising adventure. Well-done.

www.ingramcontent.com/pod-product-compliance
Lightning Source LLC
LaVergne TN
LVHW051327050326
832903LV00031B/3402